Michael Gelven

W0082497

this side of evil

MARQUETTE
UNIVERSITY

PRESS

MARQUETTE STUDIES IN PHILOSOPHY
No. 22

ANDREW TALLON, SERIES EDITOR

Library of Congress Cataloging-in-Publication Data

Gelven, Michael
    This side of evil / by Michael Gelven
    p.   cm. — (Marquette studues in philosophy; #22)

    ISBN 0-87462-621-8
    1. Good and evil I. Title. II. Series: Marquette studues in
philosophy ; #22.
    BJ1401 .G45 1998
    170—ddc21   98-2532

MEMBER: Association of American University Presses

MARQUETTE UNIVERSITY PRESS
MILWAUKEE

The Association of Jesuit University Presses

Table of Contents

Acknowledgments

To acknowledge is to manifest not only indebtedness but also gratitude. In a work as intensely personal as this, to thank is all the more compelling for the bestowals are of a deeper kind, providing ligatures that knot and weave the fabric of belonging and inspiration without which philosophical inquiry would be mere schemes, lacking truth. In addition to those on the dedication page I thank my friend Adam Biesterfeld along with my older, dear intimates of my heart, Tom Schall, Annette Dixon, and Chris Morgan. There is a special gratitude for those few among my students whose youthful wisdom and eager learning touch me deeply: thank you Tom Nugent; and thank you Mark Hinsch. Since I wrote this book longhand with a fountain pen, I also thank Jonie Barshinger and Debbie Sanderson for typing the manuscript.

On this occasion I must acknowledge my gratitude for the huge courage, deep faith, and noble hope of my dear nephew Michael Degnan, whose titanic struggle against great misfortune and dire suffering matters so much. For evil, about which this book is written, I need only look within; without those whom I here thank, there, I fear, I would remain.

Dedication

To: Jagoda and Herman Stark

and

Fran and John Mayeski

Note to the Reader

Unless otherwise dictated by Context, the terms 'man', 'he', 'him', and 'his', are used in their generic senses, and not as gender-specific.

Chapter 1
Raising the Question

We are witness to the unspeakable.

The sweet child is ravaged by cruelty. Entire peoples are marched to death camps. Whole villages are swept out into the angry, tidal sea. Our weakness wreaks anguish on those loyal to us. The ungrateful mock the gracious. The beautiful is defiled by the obscene. These are evil things, and the evil in them is real.

Some deny this reality. They stop their ears to the reports of death camps, turn their eyes from cigarette burns on the eyelids of the abused child, seek excuses in the wrangle of social cause on behalf of the vilest, interpret horrors as mere natural phenomena, and preen themselves with what they deem their enlightenment. They judge not, and would not be judged. But judgment is a necessity if evil be real. We are witness to this reality, and to deny it is itself evil, perhaps the greatest evil. As witness to the reality of evil we are stunned speechless and therein lies the fiercest paradox. For the more we try to make sense of evil, the less evil it becomes. To explain evil is to make it coherent, but it is the very incoherence of it that stuns us into mute impotence. It seems that to explain it by making it thinkable, we render it acceptable. But to accept evil is unacceptable. What can we do with the incoherent except turn our backs on it, deny it? Like the three ignoble monkeys we then neither see nor hear nor speak of it. Which is worse: to deny the reality of evil to save our reason, or deny reason to retain the reality of evil?

To say we witness the unspeakable is to say we must accept our own confrontation even if we cannot resolve the anguish either by ordinary speech or by sufficient reasoning. But to bear witness is to speak on behalf of or against what we confront. Witness implies obligation. To witness a crime burdens us with the need to testify; to bear witness to a creed is not merely to report what the beliefs are but to live in accordance with them, to manifest the creed in an open and public way. To bear witness to evil requires that we speak out, but if evil is the unspeakable, are we not obliged to do that which we cannot do?

This is not some clever eristic, dazzling with abstract legerdemain, as the brilliant brothers do in the comic dialogue *Euthydemus*. We are not playing with words. Nor are we evoking mere sentiment or emotional reaction by appealing to the pathos in images of children, cruelty, and the forlorn. For the thoughtful, the reality of evil is not merely emotive, and hence not so easily dismissed. Indeed it is the clever eristic who deceives us into denying the reality of evil by explaining it away, reducing it to something else, such as misfortune, or good in disguise. The very nature of reason itself is under indictment by this paradox. There is nothing reasonable in denying the reality of evil by reducing it either to eristic or the irrational play of ungoverned emotions. We witness evil and we bear witness to it, and in so doing we challenge the limits of reason itself. For if we cannot reason about this, what good is it to reason at all? What does it mean to say evil is real? Do we mean that things like tidal waves washing away villages really do happen, that they are not illusions? Do we mean that adults do indeed hold a child in their arms and put burning cigarettes to her eyes, and take pleasure in it? This is not what is meant. We know things like this happen. Perhaps we mean by the reality of evil that, though such things happen, they ought not to happen. It is surely right to say adults ought not to burn a child's eye with cigarettes. It is perhaps less obvious that we can say the tidal wave ought not sweep the village out to sea, for we are not quite sure whether there is in such a phenomenon any responsibility. Perhaps it just happens. But is moral censure all that is meant when we affirm the reality of evil? Would we still call it evil if the child's eyes are burned by accident while playing with fireworks? To affirm the reality of evil is not merely to admit that such unpleasant things really do happen, nor is it even to say that such things ought not to happen. For the admission that such things happen does not confound the mind with the gall of paradox, nor does the mere moral censure of an act suffice to explain our witness. The affirmation of evil as real is neither a factual claim about events nor the mere moral indictment by an ethical judgment. To assert the reality, as opposed to the mere occurrence in nature, of anything is to enter into the dark and suspect, yet irresistible, realm of ontological speculation. Whether consciously or not, whether we like it or not, certain questions lead us beyond the safe arenas in which reason provides or at least promises determinable and terminating answers, and into the more troubling—but always more interesting—field philosophers have for centuries identified with the shibboleth, metaphysics. Into this conceptual cauldron are poured all those uneasy questions of the ultimate, from truth and soul, freedom and destiny, to the cosmos and the sacred, to God and evil.

To locate metaphysics as the proper—or even only—mat on which to wrestle with the problems and meanings of evil is itself a startling revelation. Does evil go that deep? There are many topics of considerable interest that can be discussed quite successfully without bringing in the heaviest artillery within the philosophical battery, metaphysics; so why does evil seem to demand such mighty ordnance? To raise the point from the counter-perspective is even more startling: is the fundamental nature of being itself so configured that evil and its opposite are essential for our understanding of reality? This preceding sentence deserves a remark. Why say: 'evil and its opposite'? The term *good is* a fairly non-spectacular word; we use it every day, both properly and coherently, so obviously we know what the word means, and do not quail or quiver at its occurrence. The moment it is conjoined with *evil* however, it seems to take on portent of massive significance; for when we speak of good and evil we seem to invoke the deepest resources of our thinking, as if we were reaching into the very guts and bowels of living truth. The two terms, 'evil' and 'reality' are intimidating; they are words of great power and great mystery, and the huge authority of each seems reason enough, almost, to link them. How could two terms that mean so much not belong together? In every age—including our own—and in every part of the vast atlas where thinkers reflect, there are those who find it necessary to think about what is ultimate only by wedding these terms, creating what might be called 'realist accounts of evil.' There are, to be sure, others who speak of these terms separately, creating non-realist accounts of evil. Curiously, both terms, evil and real, seem to diminish in importance when disjoined, as when the word 'love' is disjoined from the lofty, reducing it to the phenomenon of propagation. Does *Romeo and Juliet* really tell us merely about the copulation of animals or even plants? Is evil merely the creation of our own minds, entirely unanchored to an externalist reality that merely happens, a reality that is entirely tacit beyond its brute existence?

We are not forced to speculate unassisted, as if such questions only recently arrived. To ask what it might mean to say that evil is real is not without precedent. In Plato's dialogue, the *Phaedo*, Socrates suggests that the body is the source of evil. Is it not, after all, our lusts, our weaknesses, our ungoverned desires, all located in the body, that cause us to go astray, to distract us from the nobility of the mind? Are there, then, not two forces, the one spiritual, which is good, the other corporeal, which is evil? This suggestion is not persistent throughout the other dialogues of Plato and thus cannot be considered a fundamental tenet of his thought—which is why it should be called a suggestion only—but there is no doubt that there is an appeal to this way of thinking that transcends a single dialogue. A more radical version can be found in the Persian thinker Manes, who identifies reality itself as the struggle between the good soul and the evil body, an account which provides enormous satisfaction to the metaphysical itch, for the body is palpably real, it is known directly and intimately; it is observable as well as internally felt. Manicheanism has the advantage of all fundamentalist accounts: the body is not partly good, or sometimes neutral, it is evil in itself, always—there is no need to seek elsewhere for some spiritual or preternatural force that explains the body's evil; it is evil in toto, the thing itself, the very sum and substance of the dark force, equal to its opposite, the force of light. Is this, or something like it, what is meant by saying evil is real?

The youthful Augustine adopted Manicheanism, and then spent most of his early maturity fighting against it, though he was reluctant to surrender its appeal entirely. With his critique one might note the first step toward non-realist accounts of evil; for Augustine finally argues that being itself is good; even imperfect beings, insofar as they exist at all, are good; their imperfection is due to the tendency to non-being: evil is the principle of non-existence or nothingness. This is still a metaphysical doctrine, manifesting a reluctance to discuss reality without reference to good and evil, or to discuss evil independently of reality; but the seed is planted. Evil is not a positive entity as Manes suggests, but a negative force, tending toward nothingness. Augustine's struggle seems to steer western thought generally away from Manichean dualism, but the east provided more fertile ground, and even today oriental thought is far more congenial to suggestions that reality is bound up with the struggle between forces of light and darkness, like Yen and Yang.

It is with David Hume and Immanual Kant that the non-realist position within western thought seems to triumph. The former argues clearly that the 'ought' cannot be derived from the 'is,' and the latter brilliantly shows how moral reasoning stems entirely from the power of the mind to command us to adhere to its own coherent nature. It is not the world but the mind that originates good and evil. There is still authority—indeed absolute authority—in moral reasoning, but its anchor is not in the physical world at all, but simply in our thinking. Evil is merely irrational willing, i.e., immorality. The morally responsible takes precedence over any power or principle of metaphysics, and the results of this transcendental critique seem entirely satisfying. There is no need for metaphysics at all; we can forget about satanic beings seeking to entrap our souls, or forces, like gravity, that drag us down to chthonic debts, or powers of darkness making us unfit and vile. It is enough that we are responsible for being irresponsible. Man himself is bad enough; we do not need any spiritual or religious externals, whether powers or entities or principles; we certainly do not need traditional substantive metaphysics. Indeed, the more we allow some externalist cause or source for evil, the less responsible we hold ourselves—and that is dangerous indulgence. There seems to be, then, a *moral* reason for denying the reality of evil. Perhaps if we begin to hold ourselves responsible rather than seek some whipping boy or realist, external spirit, we may learn to become good. Metaphysical accounts of evil turn so easily into excuses: the devil made me do it; or: I was determined by nature to do it. It seems, then, that non-realism is morally superior to realism; it also seems that any appeal to metaphysical forces as an account of evil is rank superstition.

Before we cede the modern field entirely to the non-realists, however, we must remind ourselves that one of Kant's most ardent, though critical, admirers uses the very transcendental critique he inherited from his mentor to argue for an extreme, stunning, and persuasive defense of the realist position. Arthur Schopenhauer does not merely assert that evil is real; he claims that the real is evil. It is not the Manichean's body, nor the voluntarist's soul, nor the human will, nor the satanic demons, nor the immorality of the free, but reality—everything and all of it—that is evil. Augustine claims that whatever is, insofar as it has being, is good; Schopenhauer turns this upside down: what is, just because it is, is evil. The world-will dominates as fundamental power: it creates in order to destroy, for power alone matters, not its results; and every individual thing that exists, just because it is an individual entity, becomes a threat to the absolute hegemony of the world will, so the will must ultimately destroy what the will itself creates. The only way to seek any independence from this dark reality is to escape, however briefly, from its principle of utility and purpose—which amounts to denying ultimate reality by creating realms ungoverned by mere force: such as art, philosophy, and individual sanctity. These escapes cannot last, for the power of evil is ultimate; but there is a triumph even in these brief denials which constitute the unreal but meaningful realm of the good. Since Kant has shown that reason is a part of personal consciousness and not an external force, it seems to follow that all order, discipline, coherence, peace—all that we call good—are due solely to our ability to render things coherent by the principle of sufficient reason or self-reflective judgment, and thus are representations, and not reality. Whatever is not due to our representation is therefore real, and, being distinct from order and coherence must be incoherent and disordered—that is, raw power. We escape evil and thereby artificially create the good only by denying or rejecting the ultimately real power of the world Will.

There is a codicil to this inheritance; and his name is Frederich Nietzsche. Accepting Schopenhauer's account that the world-Will is evil, this genius of prose simply upends the argument, like flipping an existential pancake, and suggests that it is possible to affirm what is now called the Will to Power by becoming more evil. To do this we must transvalue values, celebrate power itself and not the restraints upon it, replace Schopenhauer's reverence for man as autonomous of power with a super-man who embraces it, and in general goes "beyond" what is moral. For all his seeming rebellion, however, Nietzsche does not reject Schopenhauer's basic doctrine: reality is power and power is evil. Whether to affirm or deny this depends on which realist is the more powerful theorist.

What, then is sheer or raw power? How are we to think about it? Very often the metaphor of a machine is used to reflect its meaning. Being mindless, the machine churns on, indifferent to its effects, mangling the user's hands or crushing the human impediment as it smashes the rock. Yet, there is a kind of order in the machine, even if it is an independent force—which is why the cosmic picture of a world-machine, mechanism, is so attractive. Molecules and atoms as well as planets and even galaxies, move about in their allotted spheres, doing what we observe them doing in an eerily constant way, entirely without concern for those of us who observe it, but still obeying, as it were, the laws that govern them. We deny them purpose, calculation, perhaps even external causality: they simply do what they do, and it is apparently only our observing them that provides what we call natural laws. In themselves, however, they are simply power—ultimate power—and nothing else. Mechanism is an appealing metaphysics because of its economy; we need invent no external origin or system beyond the brute occurrence of these natural phenomena. It also allows us to adopt a certain toughness of intellect, unpersuaded by sentiment or emotion, thereby sequestering the distractions of personalist superstition. Since machines do not feel, and the world is basically a machine, our feelings are not only irrelevant, they get in the way. So much success in understanding nature has followed from the development of mechanistic accounts that it is difficult if not impossible to deny its authority. Yet, at bottom, the very metaphor that sustains mechanism ultimately proves untenable. Machines are designed. Oddly, aside from our own motives, it may be only the machine as an externalist reality that not only permits but demands purposive accounts. I can say assuredly that the purpose of the carburator is to mix fuel and air; and the reason I can say this is that it was designed to mix these elements. It may well be improper for me to claim that the purpose of the broad-leafed undergrowth is to absorb more sunlight in the shady dimness of the forest floor; but I must be able to say the purpose of the refrigerator is to keep food from spoiling since that is how it was designed and why I paid for it. Since we design and make machines for a purpose, it is uncommonly dense to use the machine as the model of nature and yet insist nature has no purposive laws. Perhaps this infelicity is due simply to the inadvertence of the lexicographers: they do not *really* mean the world is like a designed machine—so perhaps 'mechanism' really is the wrong word. What is really meant by the defenders of mechanism is that the world is made intelligible solely by means of efficient causes in space and time; the "machine" part of their name is at best an appeal to what might be called an uncaring inevitability.

It may be, if not the wrong, then at least an unfortunate terminology; though it is difficult to think of another candidate. For if we try to imagine an undesigned machine the metaphor then loses its authority to account for law-likeness. Certainly on the level of metaphysics the efficacy of any cosmic metaphor requires special precision. The determining characteristic of a machine is the indifference inherent in its relentless, inevitable activity: the machine does not care about us. Since, however, machines are designed, it were better to rely on the original term: power. Both Schopenhauer and Nietzsche conjoin this term, 'power,' with 'will'—not in the sense of a governed or controlled volition, but in the sense of the ungovernable, as when we speak of a willful brat. They prefer 'will' to 'machine' precisely because will seems ultimate, undesigned, even feral. If a willful, untractable child represents raw nature, supremely self-indulgent, and uncaring of others or even itself save for the exercise of its power, the choice of 'will' over 'machine' is actually preferable. Whatever else raw power suggests, it provokes a sense of ungoverned, incoherent, irrepressible and inevitable force, like exploding energy, or self-destructive corruption, reminding us of Lord Acton's remark about absolute power corrupting absolutely.

If the world, whether conceived as machine or will, is simply power, it must be contrasted with how we think about the possibility of another fundamental reality not reducible to power—persons. The world as fundamental power is not merely impersonal, nor merely indifferent to persons, it is, as raw power, inevitable, and hence anti-person. For all of the ways we seem to think of persons, such as loving, guilty, forgiving, precious, sacrificing, having worth, responsible, self-consciously knowing and not knowing, are all anti-power. If the entire world is naught but power, it seems the world is quite literally impersonal—there can be no people in it. The world would then be, as impersonal, evil. This suggests that what is meant by evil is power so great that it eclipses or seeks to eclipse, the very possibility of there being a person; but it also suggests that to be a person is possible only by retreating from power, and thereby becoming non-inevitable, denying automaticity or at least its hegemony over us or within us. In a curious existential move, then, this argument reveals a deeper understanding of world reality as power precisely by contrasting it to what it means to be a person. Unless we already have some sense of what it means to be a person, we cannot understand reality as evil, for absolute power is irrepressible inevitability—and persons, at least in their own uniqueness, are neither irrepressible nor inevitable; their existence is contingent and their nature is to be free. Later in this inquiry, particularly in Chapters Five, Nine and Ten, the wealth of this suggestion will be more thoroughly mined.

Nietzsche's death in 1900 opened the twentieth century, which now at its end seems a period the brutality, cruelty and savagery of which can scarcely be surpassed, giving some credence to these dark metaphysicians; but now it has become an existential metaphysics: one concerned directly with meaning, and not with entities. It used to be a quaint dismissal to identify an argument as "semantic"—as if to say it is unworthy to quarrel over mere words; that if contenders in a dispute do not agree at the onset on what the key terms mean, the disputation would simply go nowhere; or perhaps worse, go everywhere and anywhere like a ship without anchor. To avoid such wanton tossing on the seas of discourse, the convention of stipulation was introduced as a tether: grant us the privilege to assign provisional meanings as precisely as possible, and only then can genuine contention take place. It seems such a sane and civil procedure; for if one stipulation reveals an absurdity, we can gently introduce another. With Schopenhauer and Nietzsche, however, what used to be called mere semantic arguments turn out to be the real thing. Gentlemanly stipulations are dismissed, and the quarrels about reality become struggles about meaning, and struggles about meaning in turn reveal themselves as all-out wars about reality, as if to misinterpret what it means to be real is to fail at being real—which is too important to be left to semantics. There is no doubt that Nietzsche eats broken glass for breakfast, and in his angry presence such niceties as stipulation are swept furiously aside, for apparently truth reveals herself only to warriors and the bold. Such boldness is not uncritical, however; careful argumentation and analysis still belong to discourse, but the sharpening of swords, though necessary, is still subservient to the warrior's use of them. We must cut the Gordian knots, not untie them.

It is not the usual strategy of historians of philosophy to put Schopenhauer and Nietzsche in the context of the dispute between realist and non-realist accounts of evil; indeed, neither is it the strategy of those who write on evil to see these two German thinkers as the pre-eminent defenders of its reality. If it is not the usual strategy, perhaps that is an excellent reason to suggest it now—not so much for its novelty as a way to read history, but very much as a way to focus the burning laser of critique directly on the truth about confronting evil. At the beginning of this chapter the question was raised: what is meant by suggesting that evil is real? The preceding historical sketch, if nothing else, shows the unexpected depth of the question; but it also shows the wealth that awaits the mining of the depth with existential drilling. It is now no longer possible to locate the problem of evil merely in terms of theodicy, as if evil were a problem only for theists. Neither is it still possible to assume that the fundamental dualism between fact and value, so esteemed by the certaintists of the Enlightenment, is beyond critique. Yet, for all the importance of this historical reading, the present task is not one of interpreting the tradition; for these discoveries of the late nineteenth and early twentieth century existential thinkers have left us with a more pressing need: to carry out an original revisitation of the problems themselves, directly confronting what evil and reality mean. And although theodicy may now seem demoted to non-central and dependent status, this revisitation gives new validity and rank to the topic, not from the metaphysical or theological disputes about whether God can exist in a world with real evil, but from the more revealing, though more deeply buried, existential truths concerning what we must mean by reality, evil, and God.

To get at these truths we may now suggest a reversal. Suppose we do not ask: given the reality of evil, must God be real or unreal? Rather, we ask: can *evil* be real, given the reality or non-reality of God? By inverting the question in this way, the emphasis is placed directly on what it means to say evil is real. The full impact of this species of asking must await the final three chapters; but even now it is possible to sketch out how the existential question lurks even in the traditional accounts.

In Scene Three of Eugene O'Neill's *Desire Under the Elms*, the woman Abbie tells her younger lover, Eben, that out of love for him she had smothered their own infant son to death. O'Neill writes:

"Eben: (falls to his knees as if he'd been struck--his voice trembling with horror) Oh, God A'mighty! A'mighty God!..."

This hair-raising appeal to the divine in the face of unspeakable horror is a triumph of dramaturgy. If even moderately well-performed the audience is entirely rapt; we feel the enormity of evil as palpably and as truthfully as art can provide. Eben's call on the Almighty reveals an apparent necessity in the confrontation of the unendurable.

Only God, it seems, is ample enough to absorb the outrage. The mother's infanticide is so grotesque nothing, save God himself, can encompass it.

The play works because it is truth-revealing. There is a curious propensity, perhaps even an inevitability, to link in some way the name of God to our witness of great evil, either to evoke the name solely to reject it in a moral shudder of atheistic revulsion, or to call upon it as our final refuge in the desperate search for containment or forgiveness. The two terms 'evil' and 'God' seem to belong together, like crime and punishment, joy and sorrow, man and woman. To call on one term seems to evoke the other, even when there seems no independent justification for doing so. This is not a peculiarity of Irish-American playwrights; Aeschylus does the same thing in *Agammemnon*, Shakespeare does it in *King Lear*, Dostoyevski in *The Brothers Karamozov*. Atheistic writers do it, from Mark Twain and Jean-Paul Sartre to George Bernard Shaw. Many non-believers call upon the name of God in order to deny it, precisely because of evil; Kant appeals to evil as the greatest reason for God's reality. Milton and Voltaire, theodicist and atheist, mirror, in their magnificent refutations of each other, a universal conflict.

Perhaps Eben's cry to God is due in part to the superogatory characteristic of both terms: both God and evil seem to transcend our ordinary justifications; they are both terms outside the text of ordinary events. Both lure us beyond the familiar, the safe, the common. There is no science of either God or evil. In the face of evil Eben cries out to God just because they both transcend science, they both are unspeakable in the sense they cannot be made to conform to principles that render them acceptable to us. Indeed some would say that the ideas of God and evil belong together just because both are nonsense. If neither yield to the mathematical analysis in science, both are illusions. Evil, no less than God, is but a froth of unanchored speculation.

It is not by accident that thinkers who take either notion seriously inevitably seem to raise "the problem of evil" in theological terms. Can a good God co-exist with real evil? Can evil be real without the reality of God? These are undeniably great questions, and the responses to them by theodicists and anti-theodicists constitute even now an on-going disputation that is worthy of reflection. We can identify a theodicist as one who argues that the existence of a good

and powerful God is consistent with evil, perhaps even necessary for
there to be evil; and we can identify an anti-theodicist, usually though
not necessarily an atheist, as one who finds a theistic God--a god
who is all-powerful and all-good--inconsistent with the fact of evil.
Even the most casual visitations to these arguments reveal that what
is at issue is the meaning of the terms, so that what we mean by
'good' and 'evil' becomes the paramount issue. But if we press the
realism of evil, this dispute about meanings becomes an issue about
the very nature of reality itself. It is thus not the meanings of good,
evil, and God that are central, but the meaning of the real. There
emerges, then, an irony that cannot honestly be avoided: is there not
a flaw shared by theodist and anti-theodicist that actually makes them
seem more alike than different? Do not both undermine any authority to thinking about evil as real?

We may witness a great unanswered wrong, by which is meant an
undeserved loss, entailing suffering or death, which the mere redress
of justice cannot redeem and the enormity of which cannot be dismissed or forgotten. This experience puts us in an inner turmoil: we
must accept the fact, yet cannot accept the onus the fact puts upon
us. Impotent to restore what was lost, outraged at the unfairness as
well as the personal depravation brought about by the loss, painfully
alert to the necessity of the judgment that it ought not have happened, we founder in the existential necessity to censure. But what
can be censured if, as is too often the case, reprimand or punishment
cannot suffice? We are led to curse, and hence, deny not that it happened, or even the agent or perpetrator who *caused* it to happen, but
the very *ability* of such a thing to happen at all. We curse the world.
To be more precise, we curse that which would seem to make this
loss in some way acceptable. Very often this curse takes the form of
denying the reality which permits of this evil to happen, for admit-
ting the permissibility of such wrong strikes us as a species of con-
doning or abetting.

One witness to the vast slaughter in Nazi concentration camps is
so stunned he is moved to say with primeval intensity: "I abjure the
God that let this happen; I deny him altogether, for to affirm his
existence is to affirm that which allows this to happen. God does not
exist!" It is an undeniable matter of fact that many one-time believers
in a theistic divinity become atheists simply because of the existence
of evil. Those eager to reduce good reasoning to mere formal connec-

tors have even provided such a scheme: the conjunction of absolute power and absolute goodness in a divine agent is inconsistent with the existence of evil; but since evil exists, an all-powerful, all-good God cannot. But it is not the formal validity of this inference that reveals anything; it is the realization of what it means to think such confrontations at all that is important. What were the expectations of the prior believer? That the world actually consists of only good and pleasant things? That to believe in God is to believe in a world in which everything is wonderful? This seems to indict the former believer of sentimental naivite. The formal argument showing God to be inconsistent with evil may well make such a pollyanna creed unacceptable, dismissing God along with gremlins and leprechauns. But the rejection by the outraged ex-believer is far more serious. He need not have expected a sugar-coated world, but he may well have expected a coherent one. It seems irrational to accept incoherence.

The stick that appears to bend in the water challenges our expectation of coherence. Our sensations should not give us inconsistent information. We feel with our fingers the stick is straight, but see with our eyes that it is bent. Reason persuades us the stick cannot be both bent and straight at the same time, and so we suspend our reliance on our vision until we figure out that light refracts in water. Socrates threatens to leave the company of those who persist in misological silliness, just as a mathematician abandons the company of those who insist two plus three equals seven, or as the state incarcerates those who manifest profound indifference to the civil rights of others. In the same way the ex-believer rejects the reality of a goodly being who could stop unnecessary suffering but does not do so. Yet, we seem to be able to accept other kinds of incoherence with varying degrees of aplomb, as in politics, love, and art. It is not the mere incoherence of it, but the moral revulsion inherent in the acceptance of it that inspires rejection. It becomes not merely mistaken to believe in God, but actually immoral. It is better to think of a godless world, in which nature and phenomena exhaust the range of reality, than to people it with independent souls, which might compete for our allegiance against the spectacular suffering of the body, and which, in their existence, seem to rely on a creator. Evil hurts. To pretend, as theists do, that there exists not only a god but also a soul, demotes the importance of the body's pain, and such demoting cannot be endured. For there seems no doubt that once we affirm independent

entities like souls, the demoting of the body's importance must follow. Nietzsche is aware of this, and implores us to re-assert our allegiance to our own feelings. The puritan is also aware of it, and he
exorts us the other way, denying the claims of the body as assaults on
the soul's hierarchy. This is unsettling. The evocation of gods and
souls and non-physical wills all seems to block us from our original
revulsion of endorsed suffering. They are stones that make a wall
between ourselves and our nature. The more we speak of souls and
gods the more we become indifferent to real suffering, eclipsing the
authority that teaches us these things should not be endured. What
it *means* for there to be evil is what confounds us.

It is here that the anti-theodict seems most appealing. Belief in
gods and souls may be innocent enough until it turns us against ourselves, as in a perversion, demoting our corporeal feelings to slaves of
some speculative, unfelt and unfeeling entity. It is the enormity of
suffering that seems to matter here, and this enormity has its own
authority. What is it that would make the scars of burning on the
child's eyelids acceptable? That the soul is distinct from the body?
That God cares about the soul, not the welts on the skin? In noble
outrage we must abjure this answer, and with it the metaphysical
illusions that make it so offensive. You would justify this poor child's
weals of unfathomed pain? Let me comfort the weeping child in my
arms, for the pain is real just because the body is real. If the entertainment of souls and gods somehow finds this outrage fitting, then
to care at all is to reject these entertainments as unwelcome, vile, and
ultimately inhuman.

So deft are the conjurors of spirit they manage for a time to belie
our very senses. The pain, they say, is not unworthy of us, for our
souls can be strengthened by it, or payment for prior or even future
possible wrongs can be found in it, buying off the fury of a torturing
god, like unclean cash in a shameful bargain. What troubles here is
the distraction from the real hurt, the physical pain, justifying it by
some spiritual calculus whose software is terror. A soul then becomes
an enemy to the body, and the body's hurt becomes an orphan,
unfamilied, abandoned, and finally dismissed. If the speakers of illusion rob us of our pain, have we not been tricked by deceit into
denying evil? It seems indecent to let flourish this tarnished and spot-
ted foe of our own feelings.

The theodicist, however, is not entirely disarmed, for here, too, the arguments are not merely formal analyses, but appeals to the pathos and logos of what it means for there to be evil. The witness to the various holocausts of history find in their vast, unanswered wrongs a need. This mortal world is not ample enough to find all the spikes of punishment and all the unguents of surcease sufficient to offset these usurpations of the fair. Take away our God and who will balance the scales? Deprive us of our souls and where is our worth in the midst of suffering? Reduce us to our bodies and you leave us not only without hope for future redress, but indeed without any foundation for worth beyond the diaphanous and slender webs of sheer fortuity. It is justice that matters.

A special strength in this position is the realization of our own ignorance. An infinitely good God allows that what appears to us good is not always so; indeed our own experience often shows us that what we once believed was good is not now good at all. Human suffering need not, even for us, always be bad. Mere earthly wisdom teaches that were we unable to suffer, we could neither punish nor be punished, and hence could redress no wrong. Nor, were we denied the ability to suffer, could we make any sacrifice, and lovers would be cheated of their greatest offering. As finite we usurp the throne of God were we to announce all that ought to be.

Yet the appeal here is not merely to an infinite wisdom that can absorb all disorders, but a wealth of definitional precision that impresses with its economy. God is not only loving but loved, and evil is an offence against this all-worthy being. At least we now can say what evil means. To offend perfection must offend the least of us.

This does not relieve us of our confusion. The unearned suffering of innocents, especially when no human agency allows us to ascribe blame, still bewilders the mind. To argue that a divine wisdom, admittedly mysterious to us, sees some purpose in this, need not require that we suspend our horror or our revulsion. It merely assures us that such noncomprehension is neither misological nor nihilistic. That there may be greater reasons we now do not understand is a presumption made by all self-reflective thinkers alert to their own ignorance. It is what Socrates identifies as the ground of his own wisdom, a kind of philosophical ignorance—knowing we do not know. To protest *we* do not understand does not imply that what we confront is irrational, but simply that there is more to reason than we yet have grasped. Though the theodicist is often accused of a naive trust in goodness at the expense of moral thought, the appeal to a cosmic goodness unreachable by finite steps actually supports the respect for reasoning, for trust in reason is now not dependent on our success in figuring out everything.

The formal advantages here then seem impressive. Justice matters, and since I cannot will unanswered wrongs, I must will some tribunal which provides both punishment and reward not found in earthly existence. Unless we can make some sense of evil by appealing to a greater wisdom than our own, the grim capitulation to nihilism seems inevitable. Even so, such formal accounts do not exhaust the reasoning of the theodicist. Trust in a divine father who is ultimately good changes the very modality of our existence. Evil now seems a personal affront to the one who matters most; the realization that we cannot grasp evil reinforces our own inadequacy, but since there is a greater reality we can rely on it, trusting that *sub specie aeternitatis*, the sanctity of reason is not violated by the limits of our finitude. Reason, after all, is most reasonable not in its reinforcement of what we already know but in its trust: for what is more nobly reasonable than, ignorant of a cause, to trust absolutely that such a cause be discoverable? Does not all investigation, science, and inquiry make sense only because reasoning is itself a trusting that ultimately things are intelligible? And is this not particularly so in moral reasoning? If the outrageous assaults on our moral sensibilities seem shaken by the witness of impudent evil, is it not all the more imperative to hold on to the conviction that ultimately, somehow, this outrage can be answered? It is, then, the very reality of evil that demands we seek some answer to it. Such an answer can only be the judging presence of a being able to right all wrongs and to see the broader justification for what we do not understand. The appeal to God is not some naive belief that all is rosy, but the stern, rational assurance that only a God guarantees the rationality of the world.

When pressed, the irony seems that evil is abetted by both theodicist and anti-theodicist since both reduce it to nothing, letting true evil scarper unchecked, wreaking the dread contagion of impotence against it.

If, under the wider vision of divine comprehension, some sense or purpose be found in what we deem as evil, then, under that same ample vision there is no real evil—it is an illusion. Perhaps it may be that the child tormented by cruelty is ennobled or saved or purged of future sin or redeemed; but if so the suffering is not evil but good. The villagers swept out to sea may in their seeming misfortune be saved from even worse torment, but if so the tidal horror is beneficent. If it is somehow better to let free men be free to inflict pain, then neither the infliction nor the pain can be condemned, for it is better, and not worse, that it be permitted. To say in the eyes of God that what we endure as evil is really good, is to say there is no evil at all. The atheistic anti-theodicist is quite right in rejecting this as not only misguided but wicked. To save an image of an automatic divine machine, by nature and its own necessity churning out only beneficent things, we must abjure any reality to evil, accounting for it only by our lack of knowledge. The term 'machine' is proper, for that is the model that must obtain in this refusal to accept anything except what is best from what is most real. The fault seems to lie in a willingness to accept two distinct meanings for the same term: a species of the fallacy of ambiguity. The term is 'good.' In one usage the term means 'moral' and in the other usage we mean 'befitting the divine plan'. To force the latter meaning on the former cheats our expectation. We assume we know what the term 'good' means when we say it is not good, i.e., it is not moral, to punish those who do not deserve it. But then we find that though this judgment is usually correct, in the case of theistic justification it cannot hold, since now the term 'good' simply means: "fitting the divine plan." But since the divine is metaphysically ranked above the human, the finite judgment that undeserved suffering is not good is simply due to finitude itself: i.e., we do not comprehend divine judgment. Of course, under this rubric, absolutely anything can be justified—or, what is the same thing: nothing can "really" be justified, since the "real" is beyond our comprehension.

There is another fallacy here. The farmer's son loses the use of his hand in the mangle of baling machinery. Enormous pain and a following lifetime of restricted behavior are endured by the hapless boy, providing him an envied strength in his character. The accident is therefore a cause of his moral improvement. But even if we grant this, there is no reason to deny the evil of the suffering the boy went through. Merely because there may be good consequences of bad acts does not reclassify the act itself as good. The argument that God allows evil to happen in order to achieve greater good, even if it be accepted by remarkable faith, does not justify the evil, it merely ranks the goodness of the consequence above it. Moral reasoning teaches us the end does not justify the means. Is God's arsenal so impoverished he can accomplish his purpose only by such ungodly methods? We may, perforce, endure a hellish earth to reach an unearthly heaven, and in the grander scale it may even be worth it, but such endurance does not change the hell into a heaven. The mere observation that there are some occasions of evil that produce beneficent results cannot be used as a basis for justifying them, for the admitted pleasures of wealth do not justify theft.

What offends in this strategy is the deceit of relabelling, grounded on the beguiling distinction between semblance and reality, switching the tags 'good' and 'bad' in the darkness of metaphysics. There is no more dangerous term in all language than 'real', and we note the peril most clearly when we see what is obviously bad renamed good on the basis of what is declared to be beyond our understanding. By such cheating, the reality of evil is simply denied—and that is the greatest evil.

The tactics of the anti-theodicist also deserves reprimand. Perhaps the error here stems from the inadequacy of our moral language to vent the steam of our revulsion. An interesting phenomenon can be observed in the dramatic unfolding of such frustration. A sensitive reader of the Nazi holocaust may, in the legitimate spasm of his outrage, find the moral claim insufficient. "It was wrong for the Nazis to destroy so many innocent victims." Wrong? What an inadequate word! We say it is wrong to tell a lie or steal a pencil. This is worse than wrong. It is not bad, it is evil. The Nazis were not immoral, they were far worse than that. They were insane. Mad. Cosmically vile. But of course if they are mad they are not responsible; that is what being mad means. Insane? We treat the insane with pity and compassion, not with outrage and censure. Even to say they were not morally bad but evil is extremely dangerous, for it seems to eclipse responsibility, appealing again to dark forces greater than our comprehension. Let us not let these wicked people escape so easily from the only reprimand that truly matters: they were (morally) bad. There is nothing worse than bad. Bad is as bad as it gets. This urgency to condemn beyond what makes condemnation possible is remarkably alluring even as it beguiles utterly. 'John Gacey was bad? No, he was worse than that, he was insane!' But the insane are not bad at all, and hence cannot be "worse."

The witness of great evil abjures the God that lets it happen, denies the soul that may distract from the body's pain, denies the independent agency of a free will since only natural phenomena now make sense. In doing this the witness may throw away his weapons of morality altogether. Let him now explain what happened. What happened was an event, a phenomenon; we make sense of it as we do any phenomenon: the glass breaks because gravity induced such force upon the fragile substance that its cohension was scattered. There are no tears for natural events. Or if there are tears, they too are but natural phenomena, they are provoked by the misfortunes that cause pain, and pain itself is just another natural event. With what, then, are we left? Descriptions of events? Where is there evil in this? Perhaps it is enough to say that some natural events, including human actions, cause pain, and this is what we mean by evil. But pain itself, under this rubric is merely a natural event; it is the phenomenon of nerve endings reacting to stimuli. We do not censure natural events, we simply observe them; or if pressed, seek to find their causes. But we know the causes of pain: neurological trauma explains it thoroughly. If the witnessing of great pain causes us outrage or feelings of revulsion, those feelings too are mere events.

The enormous burden of accepting the reality of evil is itself unacceptable, and so the language which supports such judgment is sterilized and made impotent. If we cannot change the reality, we change the name we give it, and thereby deceive ourselves into avoiding reality. Instead of slaughtering millions we speak of a final solution; instead of firing half the work force we speak of downsizing; instead of caring for the deaf we empower the hearing-challenged; instead of confronting evil we cluck briefly at misfortune, or worse: wring our hands at human frailty as if it were a cause.

So conceived, the theodicist and the atheistic naturalist are hereby denuded in their nakedness as one and the same. They both deny the reality of evil. In seeking to render the world intelligible both dismiss what cannot be explained by causal efficacy and thereby make the world mechanistic and hence intelligible but unjudgable. Both seek refuge in the fog of metaphysics, in which entire continents can be submerged in the sea of obfuscation, sinking whole cultures of common sense and common language. That in everyday talk we seem to make sense of who we are by moral judgments is not refuted by argument but simply disregarded, as urchins are unnoticed by the passing plutocrat and the elderly are forgotten by their self-indulgent offspring. The truth here need not rely on fantastic distortions of argumentation: to deny God because of evil leaves us bereft of a palette judicious enough to paint the colors of censure; to re-package evil as some unfathomable stepping-stone to a meaningless bliss grinds our moral concerns machine-like into cosmic pulp. The theodicist is revealed as an atheist malgré-lui, because in his vast assurance that all things are automatically good he leaves no possibility of a personal God—or for any persons at all for that matter. The moral naturalist is revealed as a non-moralist since in cleaning the engine of theological grime he also removes the firing mechanism of a guilty soul leaving it powerless.

What is sketched here is not necessarily the formal arguments, for profound thinkers on both sides may well avoid this criticism. The focus here is on the very real, tortured bewilderment within every thoughtful soul. It is not metaphysical errors that bother, it is the remaining truth in each view that continues to confound, and indeed to hurt personally and privately any who retain a fragment of honesty. There is offense taken in the arrogant deceit of either reductionism, but what stirs them originally is still an uneasy potency, ready to explode if the spark be given. If I am only nature, evil is nothing other than one among many natural phenomena, and is intelligible solely by its occurrence as a fact, and thus is not evil at all. If evil be more than a natural phenomenon, then making it intelligible seems to indict those transphenomenal powers of allowing evil to exist. Soul, freedom, and even God are then seen as the grounds of evil—that is, they make evil real—and so they themselves seem to become evil. The torment persists.

It may seem an error in method to begin this way, talking about souls, God, evil and goodness without defining them, launching directly into the middle of a turbulent sea without first testing the craft in the safer placid waters of the protective cove of speculative definitions. Were it not more sensible to make the vessel sea-worthy by the rigors of a good, secure, shake-down cruise, defining terms precisely and exactly so to avoid being capsized by lateral waves? Or, is it necessary to leap in directly, like Attic tragedians initiating in *media res*, letting the unfolding of the drama reveal its antecedents that make it coherent? How can we define precisely in advance? Is that not, in part, the error revealed in the two views just sketched? They err exactly by defining too quickly, or by defining outside the conflict. Is it not the conflict itself that may help us refine the definitions, or at least the understandings of the terms? It is not the terms themselves that matter, but the reality. We seek to refine terms so as to avoid confusion or even outright inconsistency, but the labors here are not conceptual or definitional, but ontological, concerning existentially concrete reality. For the precising of terms rests fundamentally on our confrontations with our own morally significant reality.

Yet, the point persists: it is not the fallacies of one view that persuade us to join the other; it is rather the original sentiments and reasoning, what might be called the pathoi and the logoi, within each that confront us with the enormity of this thought. We seem to resist being reduced to anything less than ourselves, or denying the reality of our own persons and hence of evil, whatever this word may mean. But why not deny it? If its meaning is so elusive, the acceptance of it so seemingly misological, the reality of it so daunting, then perhaps its denial affords us the easiest resolution. If ease matters above all, then the denial of evil is a necessity, for its confrontation disturbs as no other can. The visit to the two argumentative views, theodicy and naturalism, shows us how easy it is to dismiss the reality of evil; but paradoxically the very enmity of each rests upon the perception that the opposing side belittles evil, and thereby belittles us. It seems then we are wrong to affirm and wrong to deny. The greater wrong, however, is the denial; and if both the naturalist and theodicist ultimately deny, we must resist their persuasion even as we learn from their effort. If beginning with precised definitions be retrograde to true philosophical method, there must be other questions that can be raised that would lead us more thoughtfully to an understanding of evil; among these the following three come readily to mind: What causes evil? Why is there evil? What does it mean for these to be evil? Each of these will be considered in the following three chapters.

Chapter 2
The Cause of Evil

The morning papers are splattered with the grisly ink of intimate, personal brutality. Vivid colors and strident voices of television's reportage abuse both eyes and ears with feral depictions of criminality around us. Children murder children, the elderly are raped, the victims are random, and even the police are corrupt. What, ask the pollsters and pundits, causes all this? With borrowed trappings of the authority of science or its method, the social spotters appeal to the rubric of legitimacy and ask: what are the causes of crime? The answers pour out in a billingsgate of theories scarcely before the question is raised: poverty, social environment, capitalism, male-dominance, religion, neurological misfiring, junk-food. There must be a cause, else the social is not science. If we change the conditions through social engineering, perhaps the effect, crime, can be eradicated with its cause. Abolish the latter, and the former will be excised. The punishment of crime will end when crime's causes are controlled.

It seems almost utopian. If we can curb the ravages of polio or small-pox with vaccines, why not curb the social disease, crime, by a similar immunology? If by crime we mean that which deserves punishment, however, it would seem a distortion to suggest that a mere social condition is its cause. If poverty causes crime, then there is no crime. Is poverty-ridden India more criminal than the United States? What about the poor who do not break the law? What about the rich who do? Perhaps wealth also causes crime, irreligion as well as religion, too much family as well as too little. May it not be that the answer is far simpler even as it assumes deeper reflection: perhaps the criminal is the cause of crime.

We ask about evil, not crime. But the analogy reveals; and in revealing helps clear the underbrush. By asking what causes evil we do not, or at least should not, mean to reduce evil to a natural phenomenon explicated by prior conditions. There is an answer to this question which is so obvious it may be overlooked, one which Immanuel Kant explains in *The Critique of Practical Reason*: evil is caused by the will. The only object of human freedom, Kant claims, is good and evil; 'evil' must be distinguished from 'bad' which is used here in a nonmoral sense. A painful therapy is bad—that is, we prefer not to endure it and do not want it to happen, but it is not evil, for it does not diminish our moral worth nor does it stem from our free will. Evil is thereby given an exclusively moral meaning; strictly speaking only we cause evil, and what makes it possible is our capacity to initiate actions as free agents.

There is something profoundly refreshing about this account. Too often, it seems, we depict evil as due to forces or conditions outside ourselves, leaving us as victims only. There is an indictment implicit here that points a finger at the manner in which this very inquiry raises the question initially: why must we always talk about evil in the syntax of enormity? To point out monstrosities of outrage such as the Nazi holocaust or the Soviet gulags seems to distract from our own venality and meanness; their very rarity in the annals of our history seem to make evil itself an unfamiliar, distant, and even spectacular phenomenon, evoking fascination along with revulsion, as morbid thrill-seekers gather around a gory accident on the highway. By means of this distraction by the monstrous, evil becomes identified with the alien, leaving us unblamed. We cannot imagine ourselves herding millions of hapless victims into gas-chambers as "they" did. Our wrongs are thereby deemed petty, due perhaps to ordinary human weakness, hence condoned by a lax familiarity, entirely absorbed by the broad sweep of the human comedy. The danger here is that we ourselves cannot be evil. Perhaps the ordinary, unspectacular Nazi worker cannot be called evil either; he was simply caught in a great, cosmic spasm which alone is evil.

If evil is caused by the human will, however, it truly is, as Hannah Arendt points out, banal. It is ubiquitous, as common as fleas; it is not spectacular at all, but simply unworthy, and it lurks within all of us because, as willful, we can do what we ought not to do. To be evil is simply to be immoral; there is nothing momentous about this whatsoever. Yet, placing the origin of evil in ourselves does not trivialize it; rather it makes our own capacity for wrong-doing of supreme concern. If I am able to cause evil, and evil is both outrageous and unspeakable, then my own moral character matters fundamentally. Friedrich Nietzsche indicts the view that spots evil as some external force greater than ourselves, precisely because, as he argues in *On a Genealogy of Morals*, such a perspective eclipses all self-worth, making us pathetic victims rather than noble agents responsible for our actions. If there may seem a touch of arrogance in Nietzsche's description of the noble, there is at the same time an embrace of responsibility, without which any dignity is entirely bereft. To spot our own wills as the cause of evil casts us as the central players in the drama of reality, and as a consequence we need not look at the rare and gross distortions in history but simply within our own petty indulgences to discover what it means.

This view, refreshing though it be, yet troubles. To suggest our wills *cause* evil seems to make evil the *product* of the will, not in the agency itself. A shadow on the grass is caused by the sun and the tree; the shadow is not the same as tree or sun, but distinct, as caused. If the will alone causes evil then the will itself is not evil. For what would cause it to be evil? Only its result are evil. This seems to equate evil with the pain, suffering or disorder of rights that follow as consequences from the will's dereliction. *We* are then not evil; it is merely what we *do* that is evil. This reflection is of capital philosophic import.

"The evil that men do lives after them," Antony says; yet: "what evil lurks in the hearts of men?" In the first of these, the term suggests the consequences; in the second, the antecedent as agent. Common English usage supports both, and therein lies a knotted snarl of meanings that cannot simply be untangled but can only be severed by the thrust of an Alexandrian sword. (Perhaps both, or neither, are evil—but these possibilities lie outside the formulation as cause.) Since the snarl results in confusion—the greatest threat to thinking—some efforts must be expended at least to sharpen the sword. The problem can be put bluntly: if, through treachery, I bring terrible suffering to my friend, am *I* evil or is the consequence of my will, his suffering, evil? Or, are both evil but in differing senses? If I am not evil but am merely the cause of evil, what term do I use to characterize me? Am I bad, wicked or immoral, but not evil? It is not enough merely to say my will is the cause of evil, since my will is also the cause of good.

The consequences of this seeming ambiguity of the *location* of evil are thick. If evil somehow lies only in the moral agent, natural disasters such as earthquakes cannot be called evil at all; they are mere misfortunes—what Kant calls 'bad'. On the other hand if evil lies in the mere endurance of undeserved suffering, whether caused by a willing agent or by the sheer wantonness of nature, then the terms need not indict at all. (It is possible, I suppose, to imagine an evil God who takes obscene delight in shaking up the world now and then just to see people suffer; but whereas this does explain a lot, it removes the problem entirely by making our existence without meaning.) There is no doubt that the actual usages of English include all of these variants of the term, and hence of themselves can offer no solace. Our language is quite rich enough to recognize and hence account for one term being used in different senses; it is one of the reasons we have adjectives. Thus we can distinguish, for example, moral evil from natural evil; the former can be censured, the latter not. But such refinement has already taken place to some extent: if 'moral evil' is accounted for by reducing it to mere 'natural evil', which is simply unearned suffering, then there can be no moral outrage or censure; and this, as we have seen, is precisely what seems to stir the passions in both the naturalist and theodicist camps. On the other hand, to say only 'moral evil' is intended by the term about which the antagonists struggle, then 'evil' is the same as 'immoral,' and we ought to talk only of agents, and not phenomena.

The causes of the earthquake, after all, are entirely natural, whereas the cause of the treachery is moral—that is, it rests in the human will and hence can be indicted or censured. The victims of the earthquake nevertheless do seem to suffer unearned pain and distress, and in some vague, vaporous and amorphous sense we seem to want to say they 'ought not' to have suffered. Here the phrase 'ought not to have suffered' means: 'they did not deserve to suffer.' Only the most puritanical theodicist would insist they *do* deserve to suffer, and so we can shelve his account as extremist, and hence distracting. But is the inference valid? To say they did not deserve to suffer *may* imply they ought not to suffer, but does this use of 'ought' imply a responsible agency? (If they ought not to have suffered, then who is to blame? The only being ample enough to be blamed is God, so God is morally responsible for the suffering, and hence causes evil.) But to say they do not deserve to suffer need not imply that a moral violation is necessarily assumed if they do. The inference would be valid only if moral agents were the only causes, which does not seem to be the case.

And so we now can ask a more precise question. Can entirely nonmoral causes, i.e., purely natural phenomena, cause evil? If the undeserved suffering is caused by the natural event of the earthquake, and if this suffering is considered evil because it is undeserved, then, whether the cause is natural or moral seems irrelevant. That is, there

seems no difference between the naturally caused earthquake resulting in unearned suffering and my immoral treachery causing unearned suffering in my friend. The nature of the cause, either moral
or non-moral, seems irrelevant to the ensuing "evil"—i.e., the unearned suffering.

Perhaps we might suggest there are *two* evils in the case of treachery and only *one* evil in the case of the earthquake. There are both
moral and non-moral evils in the former and merely non-moral evil
in the latter. But though this suggestion may remove some thorns, it
still troubles, and there seem two distinct sources of the troubling.
First, do we really want to identify any undeserved suffering as evil,
merely because we suffer? Second: do we really want to insulate our
will from itself being evil merely because it is the cause of evil? Each
of these two questions deserve at least a sketch in consideration.

1. If I stub my toe and suffer intense agony for a short period, need
this be called evil? First, it seems rather petty, so that equating this
agony with evil actually demotes the meaning of evil. If pressed, everything except the sheerest bliss can be seen as evil, since I can always imagine my world being just a little more delightful than it is,
even if I am, by my own judgment, quite happy. Though I did not
deserve the pain in the sense that I had previously acted sufficiently
badly to warrant it as dutiful punishment, it does not seem obvious I
am denied a morally protected right, for where is it written I have a
right to a painless existence? The mere ability to imagine a world in
which I did not stub my toe does not mean that such a world is
morally imperative, or even that it would be morally 'better', since
morality need not be determined solely by the absence of pain or the
achievement of delight—though some utilitarians seem to say so.
The consequence of such reduction belittles the enormity of the problem, and turns us into spoiled brats, howling at the unfairness of the
world at the slightest frustration of our whim. But if we agree that
such petty instances of unmerited agony do not evoke the indictment of being evil, is this indictment determined solely by degree?

If the stubbed toe entails fracture, the fracture inducing a life-long
arthritic agony that depresses the spirit to the point of fierce self-
loathing, does this increase reach a point at which one would finally
say, 'Enough! Now it is evil!'? Where on the scale of suffering is this
determination made? But if we do consider enormous suffering to be
evil and minor suffering merely to be unpleasant, then evil is but a

matter of degree. It is not different in kind from any unpleasantness, and the point at which we distinguish them seems determined merely by common usage or judgment. 'Evil' then is like 'tall': a relative term. We call a seven-foot man 'tall' because he is unusual in the degree of his height; we call the death of a single bather 'unfortunate', but the drowning of a whole village 'evil', simply because of the unusual degree of the loss. Therefore, is seems we do not need to identify most instances of undeserved suffering evil, but only those cases in which the degree of suffering is sufficiently rare as to induce a feeling that a severer term is more fitting. In this way, consequential evil—i.e., evil as intense, unearned suffering irregardless of the cause—can be defended provisionally.

But even with this provision, the question needs further probing. Do we call great unearned suffering evil because it is great, or because it is undeserved, or both? It is still not clear, in other words, whether we label as evil even great suffering simply because of the pain itself, or because the pain is undeserved, and hence "ought not to happen". If we intend the latter, it seems then inevitable that we must ask why it "ought not to happen". Here "ought" is used in an entirely non-moral sense, as when we say 'wood ought to burn,' but admit that green wood in a fireplace merely smoulders. 'Wood ought to burn,' however is simply a statement of regularized experience: it *usually* burns. A better example, then, might be 'the kidneys ought to purify the blood', but a damaged or flawed kidney may fail to do so. Here 'ought' means 'is the purpose or function of . . .' We understood kidneys *as* blood purifiers, hence when they do not, we deem them dysfunctional, meaning they do not do what they *ought*—i.e., in accordance with their function or purpose. To say that great undeserved suffering wrought merely by natural causes ought not to happen is then either like green wood not burning, i.e., it is not usual, or it is like kidneys not functioning as kidneys. The former analogy is so weak it seems to lose the force of the implicit maxim: evil somehow violates an ought. For in this case the term 'ought' is nothing but a substitute for 'usual'. In the latter analogy with the kidneys, however, there seems to be a derived authority inherent in our understanding of the function of a thing, so that the "ought" violated is understood as a distortion of or even perversion of the function. Can this be what is meant in saying we ought not endure great suffering that results from natural (non-moral) causation? If the analogy is to hold

it would be because somehow we think our neurological existence—
that is, our existence as the arena for pleasure and pain—functions
for the sake of pleasure, and pain is the distortion or perversion of it.
But neurological receptors seem equally capable of producing both
pain and pleasure. We do not like pain—that is exactly what pain
means—and so we say it is the perversion of the function. Is this
valid? It is not valid of 'function' if determined empirically or even in
terms of coherent systemization: nerves are just as well designed to
give us pain as well as pleasure. If by 'function' however, we mean
'purpose', it may then possibly achieve a kind of validity, but only if
purpose means more than systemic expectancy. This intrudes into
the second of the three questions, and must be postponed until the
following chapter.

Evil caused by non-moral or natural antecedents must be *uncensured evil*, for we cannot blame purely natural events or entities which
may cause pain. This may strike us as an uncomfortable dilemma.
On the one hand we seem to want to call gross and undeserved suffering, caused by natural events, evil, but in doing so we find this
entails uncensured and uncensurable evil. On the other hand we seem
to demand that if there is evil at all, anywhere, there must be censure.
Why else call something evil unless, in doing so, we also censure? Is
not the ascription of evil itself a form of censuring? But what does it
mean to censure a natural event? Is this not the same as superstitious
anthropomorphism: howling personal curses at an impersonal wind
that has capsized the boat? But if the very notion of uncensured evil
reveals itself as superstition or anthropomorphism, then we are pay-
ing a rather high price for verbal laxity.

2. The second trouble in assuming the two-meaning theory—that
evil can be either a mere natural event that causes great but unearned
pain or an immoral agency—lies in the ascription of blame. The
intuition here is that we ourselves are, or at least can be, evil, and the
cause lies in the will. The difficulty is that, if the will *causes* evil it
cannot *be* evil, but unless my will is evil it is hard to see how I can *be*
evil. In such parlance the will is usually seen as a self-generated cause,
which means it is not preceded by a prior cause other than itself, yet
it has the power to effect action. (The present problem is *not* the
metaphysical one of arguing for or against such a power.) To some
extent this difficulty concerns technical refinement of terms; but there

is more to it than that. If evil is caused by the will, then it seems no different than simple immorality. Do we want to say that whoever is immoral is therefore also evil, and only if one is immoral is one evil? We address the technical matter first.

There seems a good reason for saying the will itself cannot be evil, for if it be evil then we must ask what caused it to be evil, and this would lead us to a regress. It seems better to say the will is the cause of evil, since the will could also be the cause of good. But good and evil are not thereby restricted to the consequential effects—that is, the suffering or delight—of the victim. Rather, because my *will* can cause either good or evil, *I* am either good or evil (or both), and only indirectly is the victim's suffering evil. In order to say this I must postulate something like a soul, which is then the locus of good and evil; a part of this soul would be the purely formal power of initiating action, the will, and when the will initiates what it ought not, then the soul becomes evil, not the will itself.

This, though, seems torturous. Why not simply say the will is good or evil or both? This would mean that in causing evil it becomes evil, and in causing good it becomes good. At first glance this seems intuitively acceptable, but it does tend to conflate causing evil with being evil. Part, if not all, of this difficulty lies in the philosophical confusion of language. The culprit seems to be the definite article. To speak of *the* will is misleading since such diction tends to individualize and reify what are really only functions or faculties. It also tends to usurp mechanistic models inappropriately. The Kantian term 'faculty' is a translation of *vermögen*; it means a power or that which enables or makes possible. "The" will is, as faculty, not a thing or entity, it is merely the enabling characteristic of a thing. Strictly, therefore, I am the reality that has the capacity to initiate action, and the ability is called 'the will'. Therefore I can will, and because I can will, I can be evil. It is not necessary to modify the noun 'will' with the adjective 'evil', since this noun refers strictly only to the power or enabling of agency. If we use the term 'will' in its verbal rather than its substantive use, much of this confusion will be abated. Since adverbs, rather than adjectives, modify verbs, it is still possible to say 'I willed evilly or wickedly,' for this does not ascribe the quality of being evil or wicked to an entity called the will, but ascribes it simply to myself, who is capable, as agent, of initiating action. To say, in the vernacular, that the will is the cause of evil, is merely to say that I as willful agent am the ground of evil, rather than I as material entity cause—in the efficient sense—something.

The importance of this refinement is to avoid false reification of a function that may, to the unalert, wreak havoc in the overspill of metaphysics. My will is not some inner entity, like the homunculus, pulling strings on the marionette-reality that is called 'me'. But this, though sadly a snare for unseasoned speculators, is not the most troubling aspect. It is rather the other reduction, of evil to immoral. If we admit we are free, and hence are the causal agents of initiating action, then we are necessarily responsible for what we do as agents. To act freely in accordance with what we ought to do is moral, and to act in violation of what we ought is called immoral. These terms, moral and immoral, refer to the agency itself, and not, except metaphorically, to the actions themselves, so that strictly speaking I am moral or immoral, and what I do as moral is right and what I do as immoral is wrong. Where, then, is evil? Is it the same as immorality? If not, in what does its difference consist?

As in the case of consequential evil (unearned suffering), it may be a matter of degree. Only very immoral acting is evil; we call ordinary immoral acting (not "actions") morally bad, and extremely immoral acting, evil. There is no doubt that ordinary usage supports such reading, as parents may scold selfish indiscretions as 'bad'—i.e., immoral—and misdeeds that stem from intense malice, 'evil'—i.e., very immoral, the former deserving milder punishment than the latter.

It seems, then, that the double-meaning account has considerable weight, particularly if we admit degrees. We can call intense suffering consequentially evil, and mild suffering merely unpleasant. We can also call extreme immorality being evil as agent, and moderate immorality merely bad. Thus evil refers both to consequences and to agency. There are, if this is correct, two causes of evil: natural phenomena that cannot be censured and moral agency which can be censured; the natural phenomena are not themselves evil but the moral agent can be called evil if the degree of immorality is severe. In cases of unearned, severe suffering caused by willful agents, there is double evil, both in the consequence and in the agency. But all this merely refines usage by appeals to intuitions. There may be a strong intuition that evil by definition entails censure and hence ought to be applied only to agency, but even if we accept this, it does not provide any purchase on the opening suggestions, that evil is real. Both sides of this double-meaning are particularly vulnerable in that they reduce evil to mere intensifications of other terms: unearned suffering or immorality. There is, according to these reflections, no unique and distinctive meaning to evil—certainly evil is not seen as real. Nevertheless, the reflections in this chapter have helped focus on what may be the most significant problem in addressing evil philosophically. The provisional acceptance of evil as consequence (uncensured evil) and evil as agency (censured evil) cannot remain as mere convenient reflections of ordinary usage. There is a certain repugnance to the idea of uncensured evil; not merely because it seems to trivialize the term, but because by allowing it as an equal candidate of reference, deep confusion ensues. If we designate painful consequences themselves as evil, then evil has no autonomous indictment; it is simply one among many kinds of natural phenomena. Our innate sense of language and judgment seems offended by this wanton identification; it seems internally odd somehow to call evil what we cannot indict.

To infer from this that evil belongs only to agency is therefore highly persuasive. When pushed perhaps most of us would admit that evil invites censure, and hence only culpable agents can be indicted. Only a person can be evil. Perhaps this is even correct in the most proper sense of philosophical refinement.

But this analysis, though helpful, does not satisfy. The reason for the dissatisfaction lies not in errors within the analysis, but in the limitation of the question. Perhaps there is more to our understanding of evil than can be uncovered by an analysis of its causes.

Chapter 3
Why Evil?

The daughter he loved with such immense tenderness lay now broken on the street, paralyzed for life by the giggling, impudent youth high on drugs, whose car was not even dented by the impact. The howl within the young father's breast, fired by a distress unmanageable and a grief utterly bewildering, erupts in its singular demand: Why? Why did it have to happen? The question would tarnish all the remaining years like bile poured upon a calendar. He would ask it until the day he died. Oh, God, why? This is a question we often ask when confronted with great evil. Why? Why is there evil?

But is 'why?' even a legitimate question? There are some who deny it, and their arguments are not lacking in persuasion. Perhaps why-questions are really reducible to other forms of questioning. To ask why fire devours the wood in burning may really be to ask only *how* fire burns. To ask why winter comes may be simply to ask for the *causes* of winter. Perhaps the reduction is even more insulting; to ask why the youth took drugs and recklessly maimed the child is simply to ask *what* happened. To ask why there is evil may really ask *whether* there is evil. Does the question why have any legitimacy whatsoever? Perhaps we pity the young father for asking a question that cannot be answered and hence is not meaningful at all. We sympathize with his dire affliction, but do not give credence to what he asks.

Yet, there is authority in his demands that mere dismissals cannot satisfy. Who is better than he to know what he asks? It may be quite clear to him that he is not asking what or whether or how or by what means; he knows how to use the language, and if his wretched anguish consists in part in the realization that he does not, perhaps will never, know the answer, it does not follow his question is illegitimate. It may well be that his question is precisely what is asked, directly or indirectly, in all confrontations of evil, from the grotesque outrages of the holocausts to the bitter pettiness of the mean and venal. When we ask why, we want to know the purpose, the reason for something. The paradigm of such questioning is that asked of what need not be the case, but whose determination that it is the case rests upon human volition. Why did you wear your finest suit today? To impress the lovely girl down the street. When we can identify reasons (as motives) for doing things we have answered the question why and no other. Perhaps the very reality of evil lies in the independent legitimacy and authority of 'why'; unless we can ask why there is no evil at all.

The question why once held the loftiest rank. In Aristotle's thinking, all things are ultimately made intelligible by the final cause; even natural objects and events are explained by their purpose and their natural place or end. It is fitting that medieval Christian theologians adopted Aristotle's *telos* rather than Plato's *eidos*, for an all-governing personal God then made sense, since as a person God has purposes, and these can be found in all of nature as his creation. The suggestion is thus raised in this teleological context that evil is the frustration of purpose, or perhaps more spectacularly, the lack of purpose. Thus it is precisely because the father's howling demand for an answer to the question why is frustrated that makes it evil. In any event, so high an esteem does the purposive have in Aristotle and medieval theology that it seemed the only ultimate explanation, and this ranks the question why as the noblest of all demands.

Yet the Enlightenment, with its mechanistic prejudice inevitably dethroned the teleological, until, with Charles Darwin, purposive explanations became entirely replaced by efficient causal ones. We no longer ask why the arctic fox changes its fur from brown to white in winter, and answer with the purposive camouflage; we now ask how the chemico-chromatic elements in the fur adapt to seasonal environmental causes. There simply is no need to rely on purposes at all to explain nature; at best they are reserved for explanations of human volition. But even these seem thwarted, for it is possible to explain human action by motivation, and motives can be seen as efficient causes. The dryness in my mouth, itself caused by prior conditions, causes me to drink. Although I may say that the purpose I drank the water was to slake my thirst, what I really mean is that my thirst, caused by dryness in the mouth, caused me to drink water. The why is reduced to the how.

Even if motives are causes, however, they do not entirely account for the why since it is possible to resist a particular motivation by strength of will. It is possible, then, for the father's question to have a meaningful answer. Suppose the self-indulgent youth had earlier abused the girl sexually, and even though he was high on drugs, realized she might inform on him; he then, fully cognizant it was immoral, deliberately struck her with his car, seeking to kill her. When the father asks 'why?' it is then possible to answer him. The girl was hit deliberately by the abuser to keep her silent. This is a meaningful answer to his question, since he asks for the purpose, and is provided with a purposive response. It is now possible for the bereaved parent to act in accordance with his discovery of why the boy struck his daughter; he spares no effort to bring the boy to justice, he commits himself to vengeance, works hard to pay for lawyers or even goes out himself to pummel the worthless abuser into his own deserved paralysis. Is there any difference between these two scenarios?

The father, knowing the perpetrator's purpose, may well continue to ache and grieve, may well suffer for life this violation of the precious. But in a curious sense some of the bewilderment may well be eased. And this development is almost astonishing. For it is possible that, given the boy's criminal guilt, the father is capable of understanding why his daughter suffers; whereas if the violence results form sheer fortuity, he lacks this understanding. Indeed, the latterly discovery of the heretofore unsuspected purpose may provide enormous relief, not of the grief, but of the bewilderment which keeps the grief form any healing whatsoever. This is not due to the mere psychological advantage of giving the bereaved father something to do to distract him from his pain; rather it provides however ephemerally a concrete response to his fundamental question. The why is answered, and with this answer an exit is found from the bewildering labyrinth of spiritual confusion. That such events do indeed occur in the phenomenology of actual sufferers shows, if nothing else, two important discoveries: 1) the why-questions can indeed by answered by reference to volitional acts, and 2) the why-question has an autonomous meaning irreducible to other forms of interrogation.

What, then, is the bereaved father asking if the drugged youth had no specific motive? If there is no discoverable volition by a human agent, what is the meaning of the haunting demand behind the father's howling why? Is he not prostrate before a world that lacks or refuses to reveal a purposive response? Is not the howl a demand that there *be* an answer, even if he not discover it, to why the precious was taken from him? The world, then, or perhaps God, is indicted before the tribunal of the ultimate why-question. The criticism now must be entertained, however, that to persist in raising the why-question in the absence of possible human motivation is usurpatory; for to ask it

of the natural world is to assume this world itself is capable of purposive deliberations, and this is but a species of cosmic anthropomorphism. Merely, to admit that why-questions are legitimate when applied to human motivation does not validate the application of this
question on a metaphysical level. For the father to wonder why his
daughter was paralyzed may be the result of improper questioning,
for why-questions may be valid only if personal volition can be a
possible answer. Perhaps the assumption of personal volition is precisely what lies behind the father's why. Perhaps, in other words, the
father is assuming a personal God who governs the world and who is
therefore responsible for the daughter's paralysis. Under this assumption the question would then be legitimate, but unless the assumption were made, it would be illegitimate. For the father to demand
his question be legitimate would in effect be to reveal a peculiarity of
his own personal belief—that there is a personal God who governs
the destinies of human beings—but would not have any authority
beyond his belief. This would mean that a non-believing father would
be beguiled in asking why his daughter was paralyzed, but a believing father would not. But therein lies the enigma.

The why of the distraught father seems a universal response, not
one limited only to believers. To confront evil is to raise the question
why to the highest level of intensity and the broadest range of meaning. If we raise why-questions in terms of our own most intimate
awareness, namely of our having reasons (motives) and the will to
resist or to act upon them (freedom), then we consider such questions to be the most authoritative precisely because they are about
ourselves. They are immediate and intuitive. To admit the possibility
that such questions, which alone are felt reflectors of our own being
reasonable, do not and cannot apply to undeserved losses caused by
natural events, is to admit that intimate reasoning fails us when we
most need it. There is, in this, a betrayal of reasoning, for we expect
it to illumine that which matters most, and when it fails to do so we
are denuded, bereft of any protection against the nihilistic, stunned
by the impotence of our highest instinct to explain by means of in-
tentional ends. This betrayal of our own reasoning may be provisionally deemed the true meaning of evil.

1.) The two terms in this account, 'betrayal' and 'reasoning', deserve further reflection. There seems to be a fundamental distinction

with regard to the word 'reasoning': it first refers to motives, then to explanations. That is, we say we have a reason for doing something when we mean we have a motive for it; but we also say there is a reason for something happening when we mean there is an explanation of it. These two meanings can also, of course, be unified: to say I have a motive can also be seen as an explanation; but not all explanations are motivational. Since motivational explanations are interior to our own reflections, and externalist explanations, such as science or those that depend on a presupposed system (as in a government's Constitutions and laws) are public and testable, the latter are superior in objectivity but the former are superior in terms of origin and immediacy of persuasion. In order to say I have a motivational reason for doing something I must be reflective—that is, I must be able to be aware of the connection between my ability to think and the felt persuasion of the motive itself. Only because I can see (or think) this connection is it possible for me to be free and hence possibly resist the motive—indeed that is what freedom means. Since this kind of reasoning is nearer to us than that ability to explain external events by means of causes, it has an authority lacking in the external simply because the latter is constructed from formal, and not immediately felt, connections. The externalist explanations are also limited in what they do: they make sense of things solely by showing how they come about or how they fit into predetermined schemes. Motivational explanations, and the consequent awareness that such motives may be resisted, answer not how but why. To explain a chemical reaction by appeals to the balancing of equations in terms of the table of elements has the advantage of public testability, and therefore satisfies our need for structural coherence. But the young father's bewilderment eases when he learns of the motives of the drug-user, and though this motive is not publicly testable in the sense it can be duplicated in a laboratory, recognizing it also satisfies. This latter satisfaction fits our own nature: we too have motives that have consequences, and we can resist them or yield to them. Since the purposive account appeals not to public testability but to personal, reflective isomorphism between our own consciousness and that presumed of others, it is more immediate and ultimately has more authority. This is why Aristotle ranks final causes above the other three causes in his list. It is thus purposive reasoning that is betrayed in this provisional account of evil.

2.) What, though, is betrayal? According to Dante's account, it is the worst sin of all, for in the very pit of the Inferno are eternally afflicted traitors like Judas Iscariot and Brutus, stiffened by the cold of a frozen lake. The poet echoes a universal sentiment: nothing carks as betrayal, for in betrayal it is our own worth and trust that are violated. To be betrayed in to be ranked beneath what is advantageous to the betrayer, and hence is to be judged not as having intrinsic worth, but mere utilitarian value. A person is treated as a thing. But in addition, betrayal offends trust, often established on prior intimacy. Thus not only is my worth as a person offended by betrayal, but also my preciousness as *this* person, one marked off as a friend. This fulminates against not only a specific trust but against the very ability to trust at all, and hence is especially nefarious.

To say, then, that to betray purposive reasoning is therefore evil is no little indictment. When Levantine dealers encase a child's legs to deform their natural growth merely to evoke pity in the almsgiver, we are aghast at this violation. When medieval churchmen castrate young boys to keep the purity of their soprano voices, we shudder at this distortion of purpose. Evil therefore seems a kind of perversion—a deliberate twisting of the natural—which strikes us not only as immoral but also as disgusting or revolting and hence ugly. It is more than a mere violation of the "natural"—i.e., prohibiting the purpose to be fulfilled—it is a betrayal of it. When the young father entreats the world to provide an answer to why his daughter must suffer, the betrayal of his expectation that motivated explanations should be forthcoming provokes a distinctive kind of censure: this betrayal is evil.

It is not enough merely to frustrate a specific purpose, for we do this all the time. The purpose of hunger may be to stimulate one to eat, but when we fast we frustrate this purpose and no one calls it evil. The youthful urgencies of green lust may have as its purpose the propagation of the species, but the self-discipline that frustrates it is noble. Indeed, some very dubious moralizing is often carried out on this basis: the purpose of sexual intimacy is to produce children, so any sexual act, from teen-age masturbation to birth control between married couples is deemed wicked. This argument may even be valid, but it is surely unsound, for sexual intimacy may have more than one purpose; and the very realization that there may be more than one motive for human acts or more than one purpose for specific natural phenomena renders the argument that the frustration of a specific

purpose is always wrong entirely unsound. But this kind of argumentation is not what we are presently considering; for it is not the
frustration of a *specific* purpose but the *betrayal* of the expectation
that there *be* purpose at all that seems so wrong. (This explains why
the father's discovery of the motive behind his daughter's suffering
makes such an astonishing but profound difference.)

These reflections may seem a bit tortured. The provisional suggestion is that evil may be defined as the betrayal of our expectation that
there are purposive answers for what we suffer or endure. Does this
suggestion have any other support in the phenomenology of our actual experiences with evil? We have already noted that the confrontation of evil seems inevitably to frustrate and hence intensify the question 'why?' whereas the experience of ordinary violations and wrongs
need not do this. But there is another dimension to our reflections
on evil that may add further support to this provisional suggestion.
One of the most appalling discoveries of the inner workings of the
more insidious institutional origins of evil is the lack of normal human motivation. We understand, though do not condone, most
motivations behind immoral acts. The abuser's fear of being discovered led him to try to kill the daughter; such fear is at least human
and even understandable. Greed, lust, envy, anger are all motives for
wrong-doing, but they are also a part of our humanity and thus can
be understood if not condoned. But in certain cases the motivating
factor does not seem human at all, and this prompts a certain uncanny or even eerie sense of dread which alone may earn the censure
of being evil.

The Nazi terror, for example, is often explained by the intense hatred of the leaders against non-aryan races, particularly Jews. There is
little doubt that Hitler himself really did hate Jews, and so we tend to
put this down as the central passion that explains. Hatred, too, is
something we all understand; those who can love can hate, and that
includes most of us. But a closer examination of that vast machine of
terror reveals that those who made it work, the plant managers who
carried out the grim, deadly business of horror, had no hate at all.
They simply performed moderately well as implementors; calmly,
coldly and dreadfully executing the systemized genocide, as a farmer,
cheerfully munching an apple, lays down a mist of pesticides on his
crops. It is not the fierce passion of hate that appalls, but the unfierce
dispassion of motives that seem uncoupled from the enormity of their

damage. They were not unaware of the obscenity of their actions—indeed their trainers were very acute in preparing them psychologically to be able to do it—but neither were they motivated by savage intensity. That they were able to function efficiently and without passion seems all the more unhuman, all the more evil.

This stirs the imagination. Perhaps what we mean by evil is precisely that which seems in its motivation to be non-human. It is the inhumanity of their motivation that earns for Nazi terror the deserved indictment of evil. Perhaps in some curious inversion, the intense hatred found in Adolf Hitler is actually less evil than the smooth efficiency of his lieutenants who carried out sacrileges in his name. For, it is not that they felt hatred for their victims, but that they felt nothing at all that makes us ask 'why?' It is their indifference that betrays our expectation of purpose. One advantage to this suggestion is a kind of descriptive ranking: the *immoral* (or: the morally bad) is that which ought not to be done but is explained by weakness in resisting human motives; the *wicked* is that which ought not be done but is explained by having a certain character; *evil* is that which ought not to be done but is inexplicable in terms of human motivation. Thus, unlike the bad and the wicked, evil confounds purposive explanations and hence evokes the outraged 'why?' We can precise this by further refinement: all endured wrongs demand we ask 'why?'. Why did you steal my money? is answered: because I was greedy and was too weak to resist this motivation. We call this morally bad. Why did you inflict pain on your family? Because I am selfish by nature and do not like to see others happy. We call this wicked. Why did you torture your victims? What victims? Who cares? We call this evil. The indifference in the third response is particularly offensive since it stems entirely from a betrayal of our expectations of motivational rationality, so that our asking 'why' is not only not answered (for a lack of answers may be due to confusion or ignorance) but is denied any possibility of an answer. Whatever thwarts our reasoning in this fundamental way confounds us not only with bewilderment but with wretchedness.

If this provisional suggestion is true it explains a great deal. Not all confounding of our capacity to grasp and understand is evil. Many philosophical accounts of the sublime, for example, recognize the need to frustrate certain faculties of our mind. For Kant, the sublime confounds our understanding, which causes us a kind of mental pain, yet we do not deem the sublime to be evil, for our faculty of pure reason, at least in its awareness of the moral law, is intact. It is awe, not wretchedness, that results. Even when reason itself seems challenged, as in laughter at the ridiculous, the violation is only of specific expectations, and does not threaten our rational integrity. Hence neither the sublime nor the comic makes us wretched and hence is not evil.

But even just to compare evil with the sublime is at once both dangerous and yet suggestive. The betrayal of our purposive rationality by the confrontation with evil terrorizes us precisely because it is inhuman; yet, since we are capable of evil, we dehumanize ourselves with a power that seems awesome and beyond our control. When we witness the enormity of evil we gasp at its magnitude, and since by definition it is not accountable by purposive reason, it seems beyond us. This is the wretchedness—that is, literally, the homelessness— inherent in the cosmic demand for a why that cannot be answered. But as our reflections in the prior chapter suggest, there is a danger in formulating evil always in the context of enormity: evil, we recall, is considered by some to be banal.

But is it? There is considerable persuasion in thinkers like Arendt, Nietzsche, and even Kant, who sneer at the puffing out of evil's balloon, making it more interesting than goodness and certainly more exciting. There is delusion in such thinking, above all because it tends to render most of us sequestered from its indictment. If, however, we can all be evil, then it is common, perhaps even contemptuous. Yet, it seems there is something awesome about evil, especially if it consists in betraying the possibility of purposive reasoning, leaving the wrenching why not only unanswered but unanswerable. Anything that thwarts reason is awesome, for all our expectations are violated, and by definition that must be rare.

There seems, then, a moral dilemma for the inquirer. On the one hand to equate evil with immorality of which we are all capable retains the robust indictment of our own capacity for wrong-doing and thereby scorns evil as vulgar and unattractive. But on the other hand, to reduce evil to immorality seems to make it irrelevant to the anguished why and fails to account for the apparent need to condemn some agents of spectacular betrayal of our most intimate reliance on reasoning. The first alternative reduces evil to immorality and hence, in making it common, equates it with ordinary human weakness, and thus understandable. This troubles because evil seems to violate humanity, not belong to it. The second alternative places evil beyond the reach of most human activity, making it alien and strange, which seems to immunize most of us from its virus. Neither option is attractive; both seem plausible; they cannot both be right, though both could be wrong. One point does stand out: it is possible to act in such a way as to locate one's motives entirely beyond the borders of ordinary purposive reasoning. That is, we can think of cruelties perpetrated in seeming defiance of any understandable motive to the extent it seems lacking in purpose altogether. What name do we give to such violations? When the question why is marooned from all response, as it can be, are we not faced with the need to give it a special name, a name that indicts as no other can and which evokes in us a sense of dread at our impotence before it? It seems peculiarly fitting to label this dread phenomenon as evil.

The suggested parallel with the sublime and the comic can now be more sharply drawn. Following Kant's suggestion, we account for the sublime as that which frustrates efficient causal explanations, i.e., the understanding. The pain of this frustration is offset by our ability to reason beyond the understanding in our grasp of the metaphysical ideas. Likewise, in the comic, the expectation of rational behavior is frustrated by the occurrence of the ridiculous. This frustration is redeemed by laughter, which is grounded in reason's capacity to reflect. But in evil what is frustrated permits of no redemption since what is violated is neither efficient causality nor reflected appreciation, but purposive reasoning itself. All three phenomena, sublime, comic, and evil, therefore do indeed stun and amaze, and hence belong in the category of the spectacular, but of these three only evil leaves us entirely bereft of any redress. The bad and the wicked do not amaze, even thought they also violate moral reasoning, for their violations induce censure and the ascription of guilt based upon bad motives, not the absence of motive.

With this analysis we may bring together the two elements that seemed inconsistent. Evil is remarkable, but is still within the scope of our own achievement. Individual agents of evil may then truly be banal and hence entirely unworthy of our fascination; but evil itself, as a betrayal of purposive reasoning necessarily must stun because in this betrayal we are deprived of legitimate expectations. It is therefore both banal and spectacular at once. But do we need assume per-

sonal agency for this to occur? Earthquakes and tidal waves are neither banal nor responsible, but when their effects confront us with
such huge loss that we reach into our inner resources for a purposive
account, we find there is none, and this robs us of the only kind of
response that would redeemem wretchedness. Is this evil?

The above considerations reveal a particularly strong support for
this provisional definition, namely: we now have an account that
may include naturally caused events and those explained by personal
agency. The violence of the hurricane that kills thousands thwarts
our ability to think about unanswered wrongs in terms of personal
motivation; the cruel indifference of a terrorist regime that kills thousands for ideological, not personal reasons, likewise thwarts this ability; we may perhaps call both evil precisely because of this violation
of our most intimate and hence most satisfying employment of reasoning. There are, then, not two distinct meanings of evil as suggested in the prior chapter—an uneasy situation due to the lack of
univocity entailed—but one, covering both natural and personal acts.
The account does not reduce evil to the irrational—always a dangerous move—for we still admit the legitimacy of causal explanations;
nor are the acts in any way inconsistent with the canons of coherence. They merely frustrate or betray purposive reasoning, which is
never determined merely by formal rules in any event. Granted, there
yet remains the enigma of uncensured evil, which seems counter-
intuitive; but even this putative flaw may be deflated somewhat by
further reflection.

A disturbing, yet undeniable phenomenon occasionally greets us
in the social realm: the amoral criminal. His deeds may not be particularly harmful, or if they are, he may be duly punished. But there
is no awareness of guilt or regret, no sense that the punishment might
teach him anything, not even the fear of further punishment. There
is no particular malice in him, but for whatever reason he feels no
constraint upon his behavior. In such a case punishment merely answers the need of justice, it does not influence him at all. We recognize such offenders and feel distinctly uneasy when we do. He is
more alien than censured, for though we identify him as the culprit
we cannot in all honesty say that *censuring* him makes much sense,
though *punishing* him does. We say he is responsible for his actions,
and indeed he may well admit this, for he is conscious of his own
will. But to censure is to lay blame in the sense the offender is made

conscious of his wrong-doing; but it is precisely this the amoralist does not accept, perhaps does not even understand. What is impervious to censure tends to render censure impotent, and thus though we both hold him responsible and punish him, we are cheated of true censure, and this make us feel uneasy. We may lock him up for purely legal reasons, but his very existence troubles us, because there is no moral sense to the incarceration; it is merely prudent.

What this reflection shows is the distinction between punishment and censure, or even between responsibility and censure, and this is important, for the enigma is now more clearly presented. The intuition is that uncensured evil is an inconsistent notion: to be evil is to deserve censure. If evil be that which betrays purpose, the censure lies precisely in this betrayal. Natural phenomena causing great unanswered wrong frustrates our expectation of purposive explanation, but since such phenomena cannot be censured, but only lamented, we are in cruel confusion. It seems that the mere frustration of purposive explanation, as in the case of killer hurricanes, is not enough to guarantee censure. Perhaps we can entertain the notion that evil must satisfy two necessary conditions: 1. that it frustrate purposiveness, and 2. that it be censurable. Killer hurricanes frustrate purposive explanations but do not allow for censure; immoral acts based on human motivation allow for censure but do not frustrate purposive reasoning. Hence neither are evil; only censurable frustrations of our purposive accounting qualify. We might say that killer hurricanes *frustrate* purposive expectations but do not *betray* them. Is, then, the amoral criminal akin to the hurricane, i.e., frustrating purpose but not censurable? If by censure we mean more than merely holding responsible and punishing, insisting that an awareness of moral or existential diminishment always accompany the indictment, then we are in an utterly unenviable position, for we cannot censure those who are impervious to the indictment, and it is precisely those who most seem to deserve being called evil.

It is this that makes us reluctant to identify evil with immorality, Kant and Nietzsche notwithstanding, for we seem to feel that the very indictment of immorality should have the effect on the perpetrator of shame, guilt, or the diminishment of moral or existential worth; but those lacking in such self-awareness, or who thwart the very significance of the indictment, seem a step lower than mere immorality, and thus deserve a darker name.

But these last remarks intensify rather than ease the confusion. If we accept the intuition that evil must be censurable, then neither killer hurricanes nor amoral killers can be judged evil, since in the former case there is no responsibility that can be ascribed to merely natural phenomena and, hence no censure; but in the latter case, although we are able to hold the amoral agent responsible, since he is entirely indifferent to this ascription, the very purpose of censure, which is to provoke and manifest the diminishment of his moral worth, is frustrated. If, in order to ease this vexation of our judgment we deny the intuition and claim that evil need not be censured, then evil seems either a purely natural phenomenon like misfortunes and misadventures, or worse, is abetted by non-judgment, in which we find ourselves winking at ruinous wrongs as boyish pranks, leaving them unjudged because they are innocent by reason of innocence.

This vexing of our moral judgment by the sheer bewilderment of our understanding is no light matter, though it may be a philosophical necessity as propaedeutic. We must feel the wrangle of confusion deeply if truth matters, for one weapon of evil is its deceit about its own nature, and unless this is confronted, we deceive ourselves. It is retrograde to the inquiry, however, simply to multiply possible definitions as if they were equal alternatives, like the offerings in a display case of differing brands for the option of the consumer. It may seem we have too many definitions already, with no guidance to determine which, if any, is the right one; there is nothing more unseemly than to proffer possible answers as if for sale, making what should be philosophy into the vulgar phenomenon of philodoxy. But the provisional accounts of evil sketched thus far are not merely alternative and equal definitions; each reveals something important about our confrontation with evil, yet each fails to spot its essence. We entertain these suggestions because of the light they throw on the question, and though we reject them because they fail to provide a satisfactory answer, their illuminative insights, as well as their intuitive appeals, are not rejected. A brief review of them may now be in order.

In considering evil from the perspective of its cause (Chapter Two), three possible definitions emerge:

    I. Evil is simply immorality. (Cause is in the will.)

    II. Evil is a) any suffering whatsoever;

   b) any undeserved suffering:
   c) only great and undeserved suffering (evil is in effect)
   III. Evil is of two types: a) in the agent (I am an evil person); b) in
      the effect (I cause undeserved suffering, alone which is evil).
   In considering the question 'why?' three more definitions emerged:
   V. Evil is the frustration of (or betrayal of) purpose (or purposive
      reasoning);
   V. Evil implies censure that goes beyond mere moral indictment;
   VI. Evil consists of conjoining IV and V: it is the betrayal of pur-
      pose that deserves censure.

There is an obvious parallel between the first three suggestions and
the second three: in both series a fundamental question is raised providing two answers, and then the third answer attempts to conjoin
them in some way. In the first series the truly important question is
whether evil is in the agent or in the result, and the third definition
suggests both; in the second series the question is whether evil frustrates purpose and, if so, whether it can then be censured; and the
sixth alterative suggests both. So asking about the origin of evil and
its purpose gives us much to think about: how and why are meaningful questions, to be sure. But neither provides enough. It is tempting
to suggest the six definitions simply refer to six distinct and different
ways people legitimately use the term 'evil' in English, and that inconsistencies among some of these usages are simply a part of the
richness of the language, and since all six can be qualified, there is
little to trouble us. Obviously I can say: 'Evil, in the sense of agency,
requires indictment; but evil in the sense of undeserved suffering is
not indicted but lamented, etc.' Many pseudo-arguments about evil
may simply be snuffed out by such precising, and this alone would
justify the labor taken to point out the variant usages.

But the purpose of this inquiry is not merely to sweep away the
dust of ambiguities. The reflections that produce these six offerings
are not exhausted by the labels they afford. There is illuminative reasoning inherent in these attempts that cannot be discarded as mere
scaffolding for the construction of definitional edifices, else they were
a mere propadeutic for the writers of dictionaries. Some of the intuitions uncovered are truly vexing and hence cannot be eased merely
be offering alternative definitions. The question of evil must, then,
be raised in different terms altogether.

Chapter 4
What It Means for Evil to Be

The very question itself provokes; it asks in an entirely different way than the previous askings. The being of evil is raised in terms of its meaning; not in the sense of asking what the term 'evil' signifies, as in a definition, but how we can think about the reality or existence of evil and what it is like—that is, what it means—to confront it. The formulation includes asking what it means to be evil. This form of questioning is in itself so singular that it must be approached with a directness that may seem maverick to the received tradition of analysis. If there is evil, then what? The reality of evil reveals four disclosures of philosophical truth each of which deserves serious reflection.

I. The first disclosure is that we can, though need not, fail radically at being who and what we are. This is not a failure of some specific endeavor, such as failing to pay a debt, but of our own reality. Evil is thus the diminishing or even total loss of our own being, and hence is something not merely feared but dreaded. We do not say because I can fail therefore there is evil; rather we say because there is evil I can fail. We do not, in other words, first determine values and use the term 'evil' to designate whatever frustrates them; rather values exist only because there first is evil, and values are discovered in order to resist the possibility of partial or total diminishment. Analogies may be helpful.

We speak of a threat becoming less of a threat. A powerful enemy may threaten us, but as we strengthen and he weakens, the threat, though still there, is not as threatening and hence is less of a threat. If time favors us the threat may cease to exist altogether. Similarly, the young player may be more athletic and hence more of an athlete in his prime; as he ages he may become less athletic and hence less of an athlete, until, in retirement, he is no longer an athlete at all. Being real is thus compared to being a threat or an athlete: it is something at which we can succeed or fail, and evil is the name given to account for the failure. But is this analogy valid? Is it not better to say evil is a mere property which we as subjects or agents either possess or lack?

In the first book of Plato's *Republic*, Polemarchus suggests that justice is helping friends and harming enemies—i.e., rewarding the good and punishing the bad. Socrates refines this suggestion in several ways, one of which is to distinguish 'hurt' from 'harm'. To hurt is to inflict pain, but to harm is to make something less of what it is. Just as a bad trainer can ruin a horse by making him "less" of a horse, perhaps even by not hurting him through painful but necessary discipline, so an unjust society or educator may harm a youth by making him less of a man, perhaps by not hurting him enough in training him in the exercise of the virtues. This refinement is then recognized as indicating it may never be just to harm anyone—that is, make them less of a person—though it may be justified to hurt them. In one sense the entire subsequent analysis with the *Republic* may be seen as a refinement of this simple point: that harming—being unjust—makes us less real, and being just makes us more real. The logic here is crucial: it is not that certain properties are added to or taken away from a real subject, but the subject itself becomes more or less real. That reality itself permits of degrees may seem peculiar to Plato; subsequent thinkers, especially Aristotle, reject the metaphysics of the *eidoi* which allows for a participatory theory of reality. It is not necessary to entangle ourselves in this important dispute; it is enough for our purposes to see this kind of argument adumbrated in so great a thinker.

Such thinking, however, is not restricted to the ancients. Although Heidegger does not use the locution of becoming more or less real, he does insist that our very existence can be revealed or concealed through authentic and inauthentic modalities, and that this unconcealment is the proper realm of ontological truth. To exist at all, for Heidegger, is to be authentic and inauthentic as ways of being; and indeed it is Heidegger who shows us that dread concerns itself with the meaning of being itself, whereas fear is always of some particular confrontation within the world. That the reality of evil discloses the ability to fail at being who we are is not, then, entirely without precedent.

To fail radically at our own reality does not mean to die, though, death, as the supreme index of our finitude, is not entirely irrelevant. Nor does the appeal to the reality of evil mean that what is dreaded is external to us, as a foreign invader; nor does it mean that evil must be entirely within us, as a traitor betrays what is his own. The entire edifice of the internalist/externalist debate may be misleading: evil may be both; or even more disturbing: the distinction itself may blind us to the true nature of reality. It is enough to realize that evil, as real, threatens what it means for us to be who we are, and this threat manifests itself in the phenomenon of dread rather than fear.

II. The second disclosure is this: evil, as real, cannot be dismissed; it is inescapable—and indeed in two senses. The first sense is that there can be no refuge from its threat, the second is that the nature of the threat is absolute.

The physician reports the dire results from the laboratory test. The disease is fatal, swift and final; there is no plea or protest possible, no second chance, no escape. One day, inevitably, certainly, inescapably we must confront, not the possibility of our death, but its immanence. It is not an evil thing to die, but the certainty of it reflects the certainty of evil. It is there, as real, whether we like it or not, and no amount of self-deceit or distraction can entirely sequester us from the virulence of its menace. But unlike death, the reality of evil is always a threatening possibility; it is not inevitable that I be evil or be overcome by it; it is rather that, as real, it lurks forever in the very sinews of the world, unshunnable but neither surely triumphant. There is, then, no ultimate refuge from it.

The nature of its threat, as real, is therefore absolute, meaning that what is at stake in the loss cannot be outranked. If evil is real, then what is at stake is fundamental, and cannot be derived from anything else or explained in terms of anything more important or even more real. Whatever matters absolutely cannot be explained in terms relative or derived; it is, to use a slightly older vocabulary, of intrinsic rather than extrinsic worth. Just as we cannot say that pain does not hurt—since hurting is what pain means—so we cannot say that evil does not threaten what matters absolutely. It is nevertheless possible to admit that the *threat* of evil may—perhaps even must—be of degrees; but *what* is threatened cannot be sacrificed for the sake of anything higher since there can be nothing higher. We may indeed be unsure about what matters absolutely, but we know that whatever it is can be lost, and this loss is what we mean by evil. Reality must therefore be ample enough not only to accommodate that which matters absolutely but also to accommodate whatever absolutely threatens what matters absolutely.

Consider the age in which we live. There are make-up tests, pardons, paroles, second chances, instant replays, wonder-drugs, sacramental confessions, self-esteem programs, organ transplants, nonpunitive bankruptcies, computer spell-checks, abortion, money-back guarantees, no-fault divorce and erasers, all persuading us that there is nothing ultimate, that all ills are relative. It is difficult to believe that anything matters absolutely. Even death, if thought about at all, is followed by heaven, or reincarnation, or an eternal, peaceful sleep in which all our wrongs are forgotten. Nothing, then, seems to matter fundamentally. Yet in spite of all these distractions, there remains a sense of the ultimate, even if it escapes ready identification. It may well be a robust and good thing not to take ourselves too seriously in most of our endeavors, for the preciousness of the ultimate can just as easily be imperilled by indistinction, making everything matter. We trivialize the ultimate by making the silly serious, and we likewise deceive ourselves my making the serious silly; the first is a kind of wrenching puritanism, the second a kind of giddy indifference; both offend truth. To be able to reflect on this offended truth requires two presuppositions: that something matters absolutely, and something absolutely threatens what matters absolutely. This latter is evil.

III. The third disclosure is the reality of persons. The greater cannot be explained by the lesser: I do not explain Beethoven's Ninth Symphony by pointing out the horsehair in the bow and the resin in the wood of the violin, though both must exist for the symphony to be played. I cannot explain persons in terms of natural entities like molecules and atoms, though they surely are there in our bodies. A person is real, and the nature or essence of this reality is its capacity to fail and succeed at being what it is. Appeals to sheer complexity will not salvage the materialist, for in such appeals the complex plays an identical role that mystery plays in naive theodicy. Both religious mystery and mechanistic complexity rely on our ignorance as that which explains; but I cannot explain by appeals to what is unknown and unknowable, for then any theory that is inexplicable explains everything. There may be both in abundance—but I cannot appeal to them to explain anything since the strange cannot make sense of the familiar.

The reality of persons, however, is not a mere addendum to an otherwise non-personal universe that would be entirely explicable by natural laws were persons not included. For we are not mere addenda to the world but an essential part of it; and consequently we must realize that not only are persons real but reality must be able to contain persons. There are not two realities, personal and non-personal, but one reality in which the being of persons is ontologically superior to that of natural entities. Whatever makes a person *be* is real; and therefore reality itself must be more broadly conceived than that which contains mere natural entities. The reality of evil is part of reality, and this truth simply changes fundamentally what reality means. A person, as real, requires the reality of evil though not an evil reality; indeed it seems that being able to fail at being a person is what being a person means; and equally: being able not to fail is what being a person means. Evil, however, cannot be explained merely by this appeal to modal logic, for it is not the ability of persons to fail that makes evil possible but the other way around. It is enough now to realize that the reality of persons entails the struggle to achieve and sustain on the one hand and the allure or capitulation to lose and diminish on the other. We cannot think of persons except as necessarily combative between success and failure. It should perhaps be noted here that success is not defined solely in terms of not failing. We are, as real persons, more than the mere struggle between good and evil, we are also able to exult in the triumph of the former, as in laughter, love, joy, and forgiveness, each of which requires that our understanding of personal reality is not reducible to the mere avoidance of evil. These remarks may seem almost quaint, but the need to include persons in metaphysical thinking is not a trivial one. For the moment it suffices to mark it as true.

IV. The fourth disclosure concerns our knowledge. We dare not, if truth matters, shy away from the deep and terrible paradoxes inherent in three simple discoveries: 1. we do have knowledge; 2. we do not know everything; 3. the nature of our knowledge relies on both trust and critique. From the perspective of epistemic reflection, however it seems almost impossible that we know some things and do not know others; it is even more vexing that no one judgment is known absolutely yet no refuge can be taken absolutely in ignorance. The ancient Parmenideans (and Leibnizians) are correct in this, that to know any one thing absolutely is to know everything; but it does not follow from this that our ignorance is therefore absolute, nor does it 'soften' our epistemic responsibility by means of subjective relativism or scepticism. I know too much to be excused; I know too little to be unbewildered.

The sceptic's denial of everyday knowledge is simply artificial and contrived: I know perfectly well that milk sours and water freezes, that children are vulnerable and cruelty is wrong, that I ate a meal yesterday and that I shall die. To suspend these judgments in some hinterland of dubiety does violence to our normal and entirely legitimate uses of the verb 'know'. That I discover I was sometimes wrong about past beliefs does not, as the sceptic claims, cast a suspicion of illegitimacy over all my knowledge, but rather shows I am now wiser than I was before discovering my error. That there is tremendous difficulty in assigning precise conditions for knowledge should not at all be surprising since to seek the knowledge of knowledge presupposes we already know what knowledge is but raising the questions shows we do not, and that is a Meno-like formula designed to frustrate even the wisest—although the wise usually are wise enough to avoid despair or scepticism in the face of this.

We know some things and are ignorant of some things, but what is remarkable is we know of our own ignorance, not merely in the sense that I know I do not know what is going on in the basement of the house down the street, but that I know the difference between the unknowable and the learnable, the trivially unknown and the profoundly mysterious. We have, then, a species of knowledge that reveals to us our own essential reality, though this knowledge is vague and troubling; we also know that who we are can indeed be threatened, even though the nature of both the threat and what is threatened is vaguely mysterious but no less true. This is what we might call finite knowledge, a paradoxical term but not an incoherent one. What is important here is that our powers of self-reflection reveal our finitude and vulnerability to a threat that is real, and part of the threat is due to our awareness of our own ignorance. Hence, it is not our finitude nor our ignorance that is evil, for both finitude and ignorance are essential qualities of being real and evil is that which threatens our essential reality; in *this* sense evil truly is *other*, though it does not follow that evil is *external*, a point entirely missed by Nietzsche.

Both trust and mistrust are therefore necessary for human, finite knowledge; we are well advised to think of ourselves rather as learners than knowers, for I must know in order to learn, but my knowledge includes self-reflective awareness of my own ignorance and the ability to overcome some but not all of my ignorance. This puts me in a parlous state, but does not justify despair or melancholy; it also puts me in a joyous state of being able to learn, but does not justify euphoria.

The overemphasis of the critical leads us to paradoxical developments; it is why so many theologians become atheists, social critics become traitors to their culture, and philosophers become misologists. It is why the analyst of a poem becomes more enamored with the analysis than the poetry—an insidious form of deconstruction—and the students become haters rather than lovers of literature. These are not idle aberrations, they are real dangers with ugly consequences. When we think of ourselves as doubters rather than learners, the critical tends to become destructive, and the machinery of inquiry usurps truth's rightful mastery. The naive believer may seem overtrusting in his beliefs, but the critic becomes overtrusting of his criticism, so both are naive, the latter more dangerously than the former. These developments of the overcritical become forms of self-hatred, the most wretched of all possible states, and thus evil. When knowledge becomes an enemy to learning the integrity of the thinker is threatened; it becomes better not to think.

In our highly sceptical age the threat of the overly critical is far greater than the threat of naive trust, for self-hatred is far worse than hatred of others. But naivité can never be condoned as a retreat to innocence—the balance matters. There is, however, yet an important point to make with regard to naivité. The mere uncritical acceptance of beliefs can lead to certain forms of prejudice which are morally bad; but naivité concerning the dangers of unanchored critique is not bad but evil, since it develops into the three kinds of self-hatred: personal, group and species—I hate myself, I hate my belonging, I hate the species mankind. That this is a kind of naivité is often overlooked, and the oversight is dangerous.

These cursory remarks about our knowledge and our ignorance are not meant to show any vagueness about our recognition of evil—for indeed there is nothing dubious about evil though there is much deception and self-deception about it—but rather to show that our own knowing and ignorance are themselves an integral part of evil. It is not that ignorance is evil and knowledge good, but that how we confront our ignorance and our knowledge can either diminish or expand the worth of our existence. To hate ourselves because we are not all-knowing is self-deceit; to deceive ourselves that we know more than we do is to impede our learning. To seek some algorithm that determines where the balance between critique and trust must lie is folly. We must judge, and particularly in an age which considers all judgement arrogance, the burden of judging is great. Not to judge at all is evil.

This sketch of the four disclosures reveals 1. that we can fail at our own reality; 2. that such failure matters absolutely; 3. that persons are real; and 4. that what it means to know and to be ignorant plays a fundamental role in being who we are. It is dangerous and necessary to offer these in sketchy outline; necessary because boldness alone provides that prior overview before any probing takes place, dangerous because each of these truths deserves far more analysis than can be given here. If analysis need be further shelved, however, the inquiry itself cannot be delayed. What are we waiting *for*? A concrete insight may penetrate the darkness opened up by these four disclosures.

Need we always prefer a world without suffering? It does not exceed common understanding to make us hesitate. Were I unable to suffer, how could I atone for my wrongs? Yet even more telling is this: without suffering I could not sacrifice as lover. To be able to atone for wrong and sacrifice for love are treasures far too precious to spend on the dubious merchandise of painless existence. This does not make suffering good in itself perhaps, just necessary if good is to have any meaning. And so we probe a little deeper. We seem to admire those who struggle to achieve a hard-won victory or virtue more than those for whom these achievements cost nothing or little. The more titanic the effort, the more dear the achievement. The championship game excites precisely because the two contenders are the best of each league. Were dragons not intimidating how great would be Saint George? Can it be from these tidbits of folkish wisdom that any purchase can be found on the truth that beckons from these disclosures? Surely there is an insight here. But it is at best raw ore, needing refinement. Where does this truth-bearing ore fit in, and how is it to be smelted?

The above observations are reflections on the consequences of assuming evil to be real. In what sense, however, can we ask about evil only and not about the kindred vocabulary of censuring terms, such as wicked, bad and immoral? The emerging judgment seems to be that evil alone is ontologically real, whereas the kindred terms are dependent as evolutions on and by more fundamental entities. It seems, in other words, that any act as an event is morally neutral, and only the agent, who wills it and hence as will is its cause, can be real. We then have real wills or real souls immorally initiating actions that are in themselves neutral; in such cases the willing person is judged or deemed immoral. The assignment of censure in such cases is thereby an evaluation or a judgment *about* the real entity, the person; the immorality itself finds its origin solely in the disposition of the agent, conceived either as will (making one immoral) or as character (making one wicked). The kindred terms therefore are fundamentally adjectival; their "reality" is dependent and hence indirect. We say, for example, that the tree is real but its tallness is ascribed to the tree by assessment or judgment. This does not make the claim that the tree is tall any less true; rather it makes the attribute of its height relative to other trees and is not, of itself, an independent entity. We do not confront tallness in itself, but only tall trees, buildings and mountains. Immorality is found only in immoral persons, and it is persons who are real.

Herein lies the enigma. Let us suppose that cruel deceit is truly immoral: i.e., it is true to say that such deceit ought not to be done, and those who do it deserve censure and are responsible as agents. Since the mere suffering of the victim in itself is insufficient to account for the truth that deceit is immoral, we focus on the will of the perpetrator. If the perpetrator is indeed willful, i.e., free, then his being willful per se is neither moral nor immoral, but is rather *able* to be moral or immoral. The term 'will,' as a synonym for 'being willful', then refers to an ability to be one way or the other; it is a faculty. What accounts for the selection? Or is this an improper question since the answer must always retreat back to the agency? The will (i.e., being willful) apparently accounts for it. But being willful accounts both for the will resisting the inclination to deceive and the will yielding to the inclination. If we are true to the assumption, we cannot say the inclination itself is immoral, for simple desires surely do not make us immoral; it is rather the will to satisfy some of them that makes us immoral. We thus cannot say there are moral and immoral inclinations giving opportunity for moral willing to choose the former and the immoral willing to choose the latter; for then the moral or immoral would lie in the inclinations themselves, and the will would no longer be the locus of morality. If appeals to the will account both for moral and immoral willing then what need do we have for the term at all? The faculty is not, then, an *explanation*, but a *location*: it does not account for anything at all, it merely gives us a term which we then can use for an arena.

But this emasculation of the will as a meaningful faculty is just as dangerous as disregarding the problems inherent in a voluntarist metaphysics. We do need the will to account for responsibility; but to appeal to it as a nostrum is shoddy. The will is not enough. To put this more precisely requires us to say: The person, who is real, as willful, can be immoral, but this modality of being willful cannot of itself account for immorality since the real person, as willful, also explains not being immoral. There must be something built into the very being of a person that, as real, offers the possibility of willing immorally. This reality cannot cause or determine us to will immorally, else willing (or: the will) would not be a faculty at all, and we would not be free. But it must, as real, persuade, provoke, influence lure or entice us, as willful, to become immoral. Insofar as the lure is real, and not merely a property of the real, it is evil rather than immoral. But, precisely because it is real, and hence extends beyond the modality of willing, it need not depend on willing; it is inherent in us as a constituent of our reality, the way water is a constituent of oceans without depending on oceans. The reality of evil therefore anchors the possibility of moral judgment.

Immorality is not the same as evil. Insofar as I am a responsible being, I am moral or immoral. It is only when the ontological perspective is pressed is my immorality exposed as rooted in (not equivalent to) evil. Immorality reveals the willful (responsible) modality of my personal reality, but being evil cedes the autonomy of my reality to its constituent evil reality. If by willing—or if by "the will"—we mean, in part, choosing, there must be at least two, possibly more, existential realities sufficiently meaningful and alluring to provoke the choice: the mere "ability to select," as a faculty, lacks sufficient explanation, for we must also ask "choose what"? The ability to select, conceived independently of what is selected, is sufficient for being responsible, and hence is necessary to explain immorality; but it is not ontologically enough, for in addition to responsibility I must also account for the more ample reality of being a person. What is selected are not options within a projection of sundry acts, but must be realities: good and evil.

This need for a metaphysical reality or even entity that concretizes our willful actions can be seen in certain historical, theological explanations that, though of questionable philosophic legitimacy, at least manifest the need to give ontological support to the phenomenon of willing. The religious belief that there is an evil person called Satan who roams the world seeking destruction of our souls, may suffer from anthropomorphic distraction, but the power of its very suggestion shows how compelling it is to think of evil as a metaphysical entity. It is astonishing to discover that recent surveys show more people believe in the devil than in God, but reflection may show this to be less amazing than it first seems. We know there is evil, and we know that the mere faculty of willing is insufficient; we also know that persons are more real than things or principles, and so the inference seems uncritically believable. Furthermore, Satan makes such an interesting and colorful character it seems almost a shame to discard him from the lexicon of our stories. Milton's genius is far more precious than abstract analyses of principles. The point here is simply that some Christians who accept entirely a free will and a responsible soul also feel the need to go further and account for evil as a personal reality, namely Satan.

Oddly, this same need for an ontological ground that goes beyond the mere will is also found in another Christian tenet which tends in a way to defang the externalist devil, namely original sin. This is sin as an origin of all other sinning. As human we inherit, not a mere tendency to sin—which might be explained by the philosophical idea of a free will—but a real sin, yet one we ourselves did not commit. This is a troubling doctrine to be sure, but its role is quite clear. There must, in addition to our own personal, private responsibility, be a basis for our own sinfulness that is curiously not the result of our own action, yet is still internal to us, like an inheritance. The doctrine of Satan has the unfortunate tendency to blame all our faults on someone other than ourselves—a point which Nietzsche quite rightly spots as ignoble. But original sin is not an external reality, but is interwoven into the strands of our own existence, hence properly is ours. It provides an ontological basis for our own freely chosen sins. Without original sin the existential basis for the struggle between good and evil would, according to some theologians, be entirely ungrounded; we could theoretically drift along for a lifetime in simple innocence. The need to ground our sinning in some fundamental reality that is a part of us (by inheritance) again shows the reluctance to allow the will the sole factor in determining evil.

It is the doctrine that the Christians curiously reject that perhaps best emphasizes the penchant for grounding evil is some metaphysical reality: namely, that our bodies are the origins of evil. This is the "Manichean Heresy," and its attractions are obvious. The soul is that reality which is good, the body, evil. Here we have an obvious and tangible object, inimical to every strain of asceticism and puritanism, wonderfully available as whipping-boy for all our ills. It seems so obvious. Are not all our improper urges, our weaknesses, our desires and cravings located in this thing we share with the barest beasts? The reality of the body is the crux: this is no vague principle or amorphous faculty; nor is it in any way mysterious or doubtful. We actually know its inmost secrets, for the knowledge of our body is direct and immediate, especially as the carnal origin of lust; and it is this that leads us astray from the pure and noble. This interesting doctrine deserves further analysis later on; for the moment it is enough to cite it as a paradigm. We seem not to be satisfied with the mere ability to choose good or evil (by means of the will), we want there *to be* good and evil, independent of our choosing it, even independent of our believing it or knowing it. There must be something, somewhere, that grounds all these judgments, and this ground must be real otherwise the judgments could not be true. Whatever else we mean by 'real' surely the Platonic argument in the *Republic* that the real is the ground or basis of the true must be upheld. In addition, whatever is real must be independent of our particular assessments of it: it must have a certain autonomy from our judgments, else it is not real but imaginary and relative to the subject. We may not be willing to go so far as the three theological suggestions: to be real does not always mean being a physical entity like a body or even a particular person like Satan, or a particular, prior and inherited event like the first or original sin. What is intriguing about these theological suggestions is that all three coexist with a belief in a free will—thereby showing a deep persuasion that evil must be independent of willing and serve as its basis.

There is a further point to be made from these theological accounts. The doctrine of diabolic reality in the form of the person, Satan, is a model for externalist evil—that is, a powerful force for evil that is independent of our own moral willing. The doctrine of original sin, however, is a model for internalist evil—that is, a metaphysical ground for our own ability to become evil that is independent of our willing yet is still a part of us. It is of extreme importance to realize that evil as real must be thought both as internal and external—a point denied by Kant and Nietzsche but supported by Schopenhauer. These doctrines show that whereas morality and immorality may be occasional, evil as reality persists as both an inimical threat and as an essential part of us.

There is yet a danger here. Evil cannot be seen merely as the metaphysical ground that allows for immorality, else it loses all normative significance whatsoever. It is, after all, an enemy, and whether its enmity is entirely within or threatening from without, it has fundamental normativity built into it, such that, when confronted it must (ought) be battled. What is at stake is our very ability as warrior to do battle at all. A sketch of both the external and internal confrontations of this enemy may now be helpful; and since the external seems to fit the martial metaphor perhaps it should be studied first.

We see it most clearly in the staining of an atlas. In the 1930's maps of Europe were drawn in which countries controlled by the National Socialists were depicted in black, often with the swastika superimposed. This stain then widens as the power grows. In film and video the actual spread of the tyranny could be seen in motion. The psychological effect of these depictions is devastating. Later in the fifties and sixties the same maps were stained not with black ink, but with red, as the tyranny of the Bolsheviks likewise spread. To witness these ever-widening blots provoked a special kind of horror; the world was being overrun by a spiritual contagion of such virulence that even the supreme risk of all-out war seemed an ultimate justification. Indeed, the propaganda value of these animated atlases at times backfired, instilling not a warrior's instinct to strike back but a poltroon's instinct to cower before the inevitable.

These cartographic depictions of the spread of evil are existentially powerful in their ability to reveal how we think about such threats: they are cosmic. Unchecked, they will inundate the whole world, and there is no assurance that they can be checked. It is not merely that one culture will replace another, as if all cultural candidates are equal; the threat is absolute. We call these cosmically spreading contagions evil precisely because they threaten who we are as existentially meaningful. They are palpably concrete; their reality cannot be dismissed. Pretending the threat will just go away by itself, or that it concerns only the nations abutting the malignancy directly, is the deepest form of self-deception, when terror compels appeasement. Gird ourselves we must, ally ourselves with alien nations likewise threatened if need be, suspend the gentler privileges of peace to enforce a national consciousness, clepe the inner traitor as the pariah, the pusillanimity of surrender as treacherous. What else can this threat be but evil? And the worst fault is our own same yielding to it out of fear? For if it matters who we are, we must defend it, or it does not truly matter at all.

This is how we think about externalist evil. It is a threat from outside ourselves evoking dread or terror, and the essence of the threat is a loss not of the battle but of the ability to do battle at all. The martial metaphor need not mislead: it is possible that the threat comes not from iron armies seeking to impose an alien existence on us, but from a certain teaching or ideology which, once accepted, erodes our own reality. Education may be the battlefield of the soul. Yet the martial metaphor is still important. It is not by accident that the original terms for virtue in both Greek and Latin refer to the excellence of the warrior, with courage always emerging as the root of all the rest. For unless it matters who we are—which is what courage celebrates—nothing else can matter either.

Internalist evil is not fundamentally other than the external. The terror is less, the dread greater. The threat comes not from another person but ourselves, not from an alien ideology but our own, twisting against itself in self-contempt. Yet even though such evil is internal and even necessary for our being persons, its threat is that in yielding to it completely we hazard our own reality as persons. This is the deep, existential meaning to Plato's distinction between hurting and harming. To harm ourselves is to become less of a person, by our own making. It is vexing to admit perforce that evil must be recognized both as an essential part of us and at the same time as a threat to us. But we can destroy ourselves by denying the reality of evil in ourselves. It is also troubling to insist that in some sense there is an external threat rooted not in our individual reality but in the reality of the world. This external dimension is important lest in denying it we tend to reduce evil to mere immorality.

In whatever realm, our own reality or the reality of the world, evil is real precisely because it threatens the reality of persons, a reality which itself is understood in terms of the struggle against evil. We do not, however, struggle merely against something, we also struggle for something. The rich but dangerously ambiguous phrase 'who we are' requires further reflection. One way to initiate our understanding of the existential meaning of this phrase is to ask about our origins. From whence do we, as persons, originate?

Chapter 5
Origins

Where do we come from?

This is marked by many as a question of no little rank. The present formulation in the vernacular, even with its grammatic solecism, itself has a kind of priority, ending naughtily as it does with the preposition that gives this question its unique status. For the term *from* in this usage evokes both an origin and a departure, as if our beginnings have great import but are, after all, surpassed by what follows. It is not merely from whence we came that matters, but where we can go. Nevertheless, the fundamental question concerning our origins continues to fascinate.

Unlike so many ultimate questions, this one has concrete implications that are immediately recognizable and even answerable. It may, for example, provoke a young student to probe into his cultural and historical origins, particularly if these are in any way threatened. It may provoke others to hire a genealogist to provide a family tree, or an archeologist to speculate on the meaning of fossils. Unless we have some sense of our past we cannot succeed as reflective, fated inheritors of a tradition. For others the question evokes a cosmic sense of origin: are we the result of an evolutionary serendipity, or are we, as individuals, originally created in some sense? Perhaps there is truth in both of these suggestions. In any event, the questions about our origins, either as a species, or as a member of a cultural tradition, or as a unique individual, also seem to matter. To disregard such questions would be to address the ultimate mysteries of our existence only half-armed and without guideposts. If who we are matters the question of our origin becomes a necessary battery in the assault against ignorance.

There is a danger here. Points of departure, by themselves, cannot adequately explain what follows; acorns do not explain oaks. We may, in some way have descended from lower animals but this does not mean we are mere beasts; America's origins in the ideas sponsoring a war of independence cannot explain by themselves the vast reality of our constitutional presence now. Words that offer fascinating etymologies are not dependent on their original meanings: October is not the eighth month no matter what the Latin scholar says. It is for this reason that the term *from* itself is so richly endowed, suggesting at once both origin and departure even as it links them. The youth as well as the parents suffer an aching void when he leaves a happy home; but he must become an adult; the empty nest hurts; paradoxically we must let go of our beginnings in order to be true to our origins. The past helps but not suffices to explain who we are. Time, like a pregnancy, promises.

The caveat about origins is important for the present task. We ask: assuming the non-reducible reality of persons, from whence does this reality originate? Where do we, as persons, come from even as we surpass the place and manner of our beginnings? Speculative metaphysics must fail us here, for such cosmic origins as events are simply beyond our grasp. We must ask the question in terms of what it means to have, as persons, an origin. How can this be answered? These reflections seem to indicate a tripartite structure to origins: (a) that *from* which we come; (b) that *into* which we transform, and (c) the phenomenon of the emergence itself. The purely natural origin of our bodies, following this development, would be womb, infancy, and birth. The womb is that which, in leaving, we achieve independence as an infant; the birth itself is the transition from womb to infancy. If we apply this triadic unfolding of origin to the existential question of what it means to emerge as personal realities we can suggest that (a) is innocence, (b) is autonomy and (c), though difficult to isolate with a single name may perhaps best be approached by a metaphoric use of the term *weaning*. From innocence we are weaned to autonomous responsibility. Of the three stages, by far the most deserving of reflection is the existential phenomenon of weaning, for it is in this phenomenon that the disclosure of our origin is revealed.

In both its literal and metaphoric uses the term *wean* implies a gradual, even gentle, removal from dependence, together with a reluctance or resistance to this withdrawal. It is thus a muted pain, in which what is left behind retains an allure holding us back, and the promised independence lures forward, urging us onward. There is also in weaning a sense of inevitability or at least natural rightness; there seems an unhealthy perversion in letting a child suckle too long; the pleasure for mother and child beyond a certain duration takes on the shadowy character of unsanctioned indulgence, distorting the current of nature. At the same time a harsh and abrupt withdrawal seems cruel, perhaps even fatally dangerous. In some cases weaning may entail a certain duplicity in the sense of a placebo, as a physician may wean a patient from dependence on an addictive drug by a subtle diminishment of dosage unrealized by the sufferer. Weaning thus takes place in full realization of the attraction inherent in the stasis of contentment that contends with needful withdrawal.

If, in the existential language of the inquiry, we achieve our reality only through a weaning from innocence, we must then realize both the charm and the danger in innocence.

The danger is a familiar one. Naivité and nostalgia are both distortions in which what is innocent is considered the paradigm for moral goodness. The sweet child, in its purity and freshness, is treasured as saintly or even God-like, unscratched by even the smallest thorn, the perfect human being. We look upon our own experience and maturity as sadly necessary defenses against an encroaching, wicked world; the loss of innocence is perceived as a retreat from primeval sweetness. The confusion here lies in identifying the impossibility of wrongdoing with the achievement of goodness. The innocent cannot be wicked, but this simply renders the child amoral. The serious delusion here is not that we may misjudge the child, but that in assuming the child to be paradigmatically good we distort what goodness means. Achingly, we may long for a return to simplicity and childhood, but realizing we cannot return, we place goodness entirely out of reach.

There are many attitudes that help us become indifferent to our moral struggle, but the idealization of goodness as innocence is one of the most pernicious. Why strive to achieve what is forever lost? If goodness is mere innocence then we can never return to it, nor should we even try. Furthermore, to identify innocence as morally good seems to equate the saint with the stupid, an equation lethal to all moral instruction. The youthful then arrogantly assure themselves they are simply too clever to be good, and the so-called "good" are too stupid to arrange their own self-interest. It is then bad to be good and good to be bad. We seem, under the influence of this distortion, to forget that innocence is negative; its etymology means "not to know." Should we really praise moral ignorance? Indeed, this fallacy is often used on the loftiest level of thought: God himself is judged to be innocent—that is, like a child, incapable of evil—rather than morally significant, which means overcoming, by effort, the lure to do what is wrong. If God is all-good the one thing he cannot be is innocent.

Yet, in spite of these caveats, there is doubtless much that is charming and attractive about innocence; though this charm may well be more in innocence perceived than in innocence endured. Children in their innocence are precious; their very vulnerability and the prolixity of their dependence on us awakens a powerful urge to protect, and as protected, we care about them as ours. What is of existential significance here is that the worth of the innocent child does not depend upon moral success. Precisely because we cannot judge the very young child on moral terms at all we see that merely to exist matters on its own, so that morality cannot exhaust our worth. Even when the child matures into a youngster and is capable of some degree of fault, this recollection of innocence persists; we love our children simply because they are ours even if they are bad. There is also in innocence a freshness to our own experience which we, as adults, vicariously re-learn. Watching children discover the world allows us, through the vicarage of preciousness, to awaken the awe and wonder of revisited learning.

The very fact that non-moral worth is isolated in such phenomena is of enormous import in this reflection on our origins. For, if it is possible to be of worth in a non-moral way, as innocence obviously is, then that existential worth must somehow carry over into our moral reality. Even as adults our worth is not reducible to our moral rectitude, else we could neither forgive nor be forgiven. This origin persists; we do not lose this existential worth when we commit our first moral transgression. The preciousness in the perceived innocence of children thus illuminates a fundamental truth about our reality: the struggle with good and evil presupposes the existential worth of the agent above and beyond the achievement of moral success.

Innocence, however, is yet a propadeutic. The child is precious not only because it is now blameless, but because it is becoming a person. This becoming is a species of learning in which what we learn is to become ourselves. Children seem designed by nature to learn prodigiously, and this very learning to become our own reality is a fundamental part of innocence. Thus innocence seeks to destroy itself by the very ability to learn, which is an essential part of being innocent. There is, in the existential understanding of innocence, a process of becoming non-innocent. To pretend innocence is a mere state of being precious therefore distracts, for it is part of the very essence of innocence to learn, and this learning must transcend its beginning.

The scenario of this transcendence is weaning. It may seem odd that what innocence achieves is non-innocence, and odder still that the ability to become evil is actually an advance on our emerging reality. Once it is recognized that goodness itself emerges as a possibility only in the achievement of this ability, the development from innocence to personal reality seems justifiable. To designate this as weaning, however, needs further reflection.

The purpose of all weaning is the achievement of independence, from cutting the umbilical cord to cutting the apron strings. But this emergence into autonomy is accomplished only by overcoming a powerful lure that, if left unchallenged, would forever hold us back. There is, if you will, a great power that, like an overly protective parent, would keep us from self-achievement; and this power must be met with a counter-power sufficient to extract us from our beginnings. In the literal sense of weaning, this power is simply growth, which is a part of nature itself; but in the metaphoric sense in which the range of discourse is existential meaning, the power is a kind of violence to our normal thinking. The innocent is physically vulnerable but morally invulnerable; the adult becomes to some degree physically invulnerable—independent—but morally vulnerable. The paradox is that in order to be moral at all we must be morally vulnerable. Hence, as morally invulnerable, innocence attracts as a powerful absolute, and its lure is not inevitably overcome. The counter-power to this absolute is weaning in the special existential sense of ceding. That is, we yield the birthright of impregnable worth—the existential absolute of the worth in an innocent child—in order to achieve the pregnable worth of being able to fail. We cede power in order to gain autonomous authority. This is not a mere one-time event in the development of a growing child, but a constant, necessary resistance to the lure of absolute innocence.

An example less literal may prove enlightening. We may note in an extended history of a people a certain development toward liberty. Kings were once necessarily autocratic to control the rapine and enslavement of land-owners, but their power begins to erode as parliaments, both gentry and common, become indispensable. Over centuries the people themselves become more self-consciously democratic, learning to participate in, without seizing control over, various governmental procedures. Sovereigns, however, are retained. Curiously, the king's ceding of autocratic power may actually increase his strength and certainly his authority. Unhappy experiments with anarchistic, simplistic, democracies themselves show a growth in liberty when the citizen willfully cedes absolute anarchy and in yielding provides for greater liberty in the establishment of order through government. There is nothing outstanding in this; we merely learn that ceding the absolute may strengthen reality. The more I fight to control the fractious horse or the complex machine, the more frustrated I become in achieving success; when I learn not to fight the forces, but let them help me to accomplish things, hitherto unrealized levels of success may well be achieved. Weaning can therefore be from the absolute, such as absolute moral invulnerability (innocence) or absolutist power in autocracy, or absolute trust in parental protection. What is gained in such weaning can be seen as the achievement of our reality as persons.

Yet the person we become is always an emergent reality from absolutist innocence. We can never change this, that once we were innocent. The stamp of this existential absolute can never be overcome; indeed the entire history of the transition or weaning itself persists, so that the gradual emancipation from infant to child, to youngster, to adolescent, to adult remains an essential part of us even as it is surpassed by the transformation. Who we are remains in part answerable in terms of how we are transformed by the phenomenon of weaning-learning.

What we learn in this weaning is evil. We begin with evil confronted, then evil recognized (as in ourselves) and finally evil combated in the struggle that alone constitutes our transformation from innocence. But this very development remains as an inescapable and persistent form to our becoming who we are. We are not merely the finished product, as if innocence were but scaffolding around the emerging cathedral of maturity that, once built, is discarded as a mere means to an end. Rather, the inheritance of our absolute innocence as origin becomes a necessary part of our reality as combatants with good and evil. What does this mean?

To be innocent is both positive and negative. Negative innocence is the inability to be held responsible for wrong-doing; positive innocence is the preciousness that is found in the realization that who we are matters independently of behavior. It is the positive sense of innocence that persists into maturity, and is evidence in the palpable phenomenon of forgiveness. I am forgiven solely because who I am—my existential worth—is independent of what I do. At the same time, however, this independence is not absolute, for I can fail even existentially, by diminishment; though this diminishment is not due merely to moral failures else it would not be independent at all. The key emergent realization here is this: what it means to be able to do bad things necessarily must include the possibility, but never the necessity, of being forgiven. The converse is also true: being able to be forgiven necessarily includes the ability to do what is right and what is wrong. Evil therefore emerges, not as the mere violation of what is moral, but the existential diminishment of our worth as persons; and one of the most persistent ways in which this diminishment occurs is the denial of the reality of evil.

The origin of the reality of persons is therefore innocence transformed, from negative to positive innocence. Even in my most wicked moments I realize that, as once innocent, now weaned, I am responsible for my own being good and bad, but also am able to plea for pardon on the basis of who I am. In being responsible at all I reject the negativity of innocence; in being able to be forgiven I retain the inheritance of positive innocence. But I am not only bad but also evil when the existential worth of my inheritance is diminished. Forgiveness may always be denied, for unless it is a bestowal it is required, which would make it no longer forgiveness. Nevertheless, it is possible to consider the basis of why forgiveness would be denied, and such a ground might well be the loss of positive innocence, i.e., the diminishment or eclipse of existential worth.

The weaning from negative innocence transforms us from the absolute refuge of moral invulnerability to the reality of persons. Innocence is therefore the origin of our reality. The transformation itself is a yielding of that absolute security of innocence which would keep us morally impregnable were it not overcome. But becoming morally vulnerable also opens up the curiously anti-moral possibility of forgiveness, which is a mirror of our earlier innocence, showing that, in order to be morally significant, we must also be existentially independent of the grim absolute of morality, by means of the inherited (from our origin) worth of who we are. The transformational weaning is thus a painful surrender of two absolutes: the absolute of moral invulnerability in original innocence and the absolute authority of moral censure. In becoming able to be guilty, which severs us from the originary absolute of innocence, we also become able to be forgiven, which surpasses the absolute of morality.

Existential weaning thus expands the dimensions of our meaning beyond the two absolutes, innocence and morality. In no way does this weaning either weaken or lessen what is absolute, nor does it even suggest any degree or relativity or softness of the moral law. We are still absolutely responsible for violations of absolute moral laws; but our worth is not exhausted by this responsibility.

To argue, as we are doing here, that the ground of existential worth, which alone provides the intelligibility of forgiveness, is rooted in originary innocence, may seem odd. But when we reflect on the sameness of innocent preciousness and the preciousness which grounds forgiveness, the illuminative power of our origin becomes possible. Only in this way can our origin as innocence have any significance in our post-innocent reality. Even more importantly, however, we are now able to sense that it is our very origin that allows for the all-important distinction between the morally wrong and true evil. For now evil becomes grounded in existential reality: it can now be suggested that evil is the erosion, diminishment, or even total eclipse, of our own origin. That is, evil is the enemy of our existential, and not merely our moral, worth. Evil is therefore existentially real.

The existential reality of persons has its origin then, in an absolute innocence that is transformed by ceding its protection for the sake of meaningful vulnerability in the confrontation with real evil. What is ceded is omnipotent blindness to the reality we are becoming; but the heritage of this origin persists beyond this ceding in the reality of existential worth that allows for forgiveness just because who we are matters more than what we do. There is more reality in overcoming absolute assurance than in the innocent security of not knowing.

What matters here is the realization that our origin transforms by yielding innocence as an absolute. We become real as we depart the security of our impregnable origin. It is this very realization that allows us now to turn this insight on the earlier noted linkage between the notions of evil and the divine. All theological reasoning ought, by right, to take place in the existential realm; and in the present discussion the best we can do is provide a rational suggestion, not yet a proof by any means. But since the question of evil seems, as we have noted earlier, to evoke some reference or appeal to God, it would be derelict not to consider the possible isomorphism or at least analogy between the origin of ourselves as persons and the origin of the existentially significant universe.

Theologians often speak of the creation of the physical world as the beginning of all things. This, however, is a profound mistake that stems from mechanistic metaphysics. For it is not the creation of a myriad of galaxies, now thought of as little more than collections of gases and rock, but the self-creation of the prime person that matters absolutely and that must precede the establishment and forming of physical objects and the necessary generation of temporally succeeding events, and hence time itself. To speak of any primeval creation is vexing because of our temporal language; we must use terms such as *first, before,* and *after* even though such language is, strictly, inappropriate. If we remind ourselves that such terms have purely formal meanings, we may avoid the censure of inappropriate usage; but the difficulty still lingers. We must speak in our own tongue, however, and a certain tolerance may be assumed of a generous reader. We then hesitantly suggest that "prior" to the creating of the physical world, the supreme act is the self-creating of the original person. This must be considered carefully.

Creating has two forms: making, and letting be. We can make (create) a table out of wood, or we can let the truth of suffering be manifest in a tragedy, thereby creating an art-work. The latter sense can be applied to God's letting himself become a person. This does not, as might seem, require that first there was a non-personal God that somehow then appropriated person-like qualities. There is no God except a personal God. But what is abandoned in the self-creating of the original person just is the absolute power (i.e., existential nothingness) of inevitability. Such power does not pre-exist this self-creation; it becomes real only as a rejection in the fundamental act of letting reality become, as treachery becomes possible only in the priority of trust. First, reality must be personal and self-created, and its essence is the emergence out of inevitability. To become is to withdraw from absolute invulnerability to the self-willed ceding of blind and total power to the more real letting-be of authority. Just as we achieve our own reality in the ceding of absolute innocence, so God becomes a person by ceding (or rejecting) absolute power. Our becoming, however, is dependent; God's is independent. His self-creating is fundamental reality, far more awesome and wondrous than any creation of the mere physical universe. But in this ceding of inevitability emerges goodness, and this goodness counters the now-emergent possibility of radical failure, evil, which seeks to destroy this emerging, and returning to total power or nothingness. God is that being for whom the greatest evil is the greatest possibility, constantly being rejected only by supreme effort. What is rejected in this primeval act of self-becoming is absolute power—i.e., nothingness. The rejection of this threatening evil is by a supreme effort which Christians call love.

To mention Christians, however, is to confront an angry protest from their theologians, who insist God must be all-wise, all-mighty, and all-good. Are these qualities here denied? Not necessarily; though what these attributes mean surely requires rethinking. Once it is realized it is mightier to let the world become than to make it; once we realize that goodness lets a person be, and is essentially the struggle against a real evil understood as raw power; once wisdom is seen as requiring personal judgment in the learning of truth; under these presuppositions the theological ascriptions of the three terms is possible.

Could God, then, have stopped the earthquake? Perhaps not, given he is a person and not a machine. Perhaps even: he must not, given he is a person. To create a "perfect" world—i.e., a world without flaw—is to create (make) a world impossible for persons. The truly "perfect" world is one in which being a person flourishes. To create a real world (letting it become) is to demand that possibilities of failure be real, hence persons can be real. We call God almighty because there is simply nothing greater than this—to let a world of persons become. Does God know everything? Perhaps; but letting the secrets of others be hidden may also be his privilege. He still is wise enough to judge—but judgment is not absolute determination. We cannot think of persons as if they were machines.

Herein lies the deep and troubling paradox of christianity: the tension between metaphysical theologians and the scripturally devout. The message of this strange but great religion inherited from its sacred texts seems to the critical mind highly anthropomorphic. But how could it be other than anthropomorphic when we are told we are made in God's image, that he is as a father, that he loves? The counter danger is "mechomorphism," where all things are explained in terms of the automatic. This tension will remain since our own powers of thinking are designed to make things sensible in both ways. These reflections are not so bold as to determine how these ways interrelate, but merely to point out that metaphysics need not be only of one sort. But that is enough to save the christian from naive contradictions stemming from the problem of evil.

Does the claim that, as a person, perhaps God cannot stop the earthquake mean he cannot intercede in any way? The argument does not claim this. Indeed, it must leave such questions unanswered, since to answer with absolute terms of automatic reaction based on algorithmic reasoning is to think as a mechanist when we ought to think as a person about persons. Can we ever determine when and whether God can or ought to intervene? He would not be a person were this so. Do these answers satisfy our desire to know? They do not and cannot; they do, however, show it is not self-contradictory to think in this way. Yet there is far greater wisdom here than in making compatible the theological and the religious elements within one great religion, Christianity. It reveals much about how we think, without contradicting ourselves, and about evil. It is a small achievement indeed to make one metaphysical account consistent with itself by redefining terms. Apologists of every type, and even sophists of the vilest type, do this constantly, and receive fleeting esteem by the unlettered when they do. This is not an effort in compatabilism; it is an attempt to think through the possibility of the following as true: (1) that evil is real; (2) that the non-reducible reality of persons is more fundamental than mechanistic principles about materialistic entitles, (3) that the non-reducible reality of persons requires the reality of evil; (4) that persons as persons must struggle with the reality of evil; (5) that evil threatens not only our moral but also our existential worth; (6) that *if* there is a non-reducible reality of person, its origin is in innocence, and its transformation surpasses this origin, but retains its stamp in the ability to be forgiven. These six points *may* require the assumption of a personal God as described, but they are certainly at least compatible with such a God.

The origin of the universe cannot be known scientifically, nor even by traditional (speculative) metaphysics. But the existential reflections on what it means to be in the universe as beings with origins can be carried out independently of either science of speculative metaphysics. The beginning of wisdom, as Plato and others, especially Kant, has noted, is the realization of what we can and cannot know. Our own existential reality is available for critical and refined reflection; and from these reflections much that is rich in meaning can be discerned in its truth. To allow purely speculative accounts of our origins as metaphysical entities, which are always suspect and tentative at best, to impede our existential reflection about what it means to be who we are is simply folly. Indeed, it is fatal folly since it sacrifices that truth of what it means to be on the altar of impossible, mechanistic speculations.

Whatever reality means, it must at least satisfy these requirements: (1) it cannot be a mere creation of our minds, as is a pegasus or unicorn; (2) it is the ground of the true, as the reality of the storm makes it true that it is raining.

Evil is real because it does not depend on our assessment, either cognitively or emotively; it is also real because there is truth in our existential understanding of ourselves as transformed innocence struggling against that which threatens us with total eclipse of our worth, both morally and existentially. The origin of persons as innocence carries over into post-innocent responsibility in the form of existential preciousness which allows for forgiveness. If, then, we wish to distinguish mere immorality (which is contributive to but not determinative of evil) from evil itself, we say the immoral can be forgiven but the truly evil cannot. The reason for saying this is that true evil eclipses not only our moral worth but our existential worth. Some religions argue, for example, that despair is the worst sin of all, for it closes off all hope of redemption. In this sense it should be obvious that despair is not the mere passing feelings that are experiences of despairing, for all of us have probably gone through such agonies and have re-established some remnant of hope after a dark period. Whether this theological account is correct can be left unsettled; it is enough to see that even some theology distinguishes mere immorality from total evil, and that such evil puts us in the parlous state of non-redemption.

We learn about our origin in innocence retroactively. The innocent child is unaware of innocence. Origins are by definition understandable only in retrospect, for origins *begin*. What they begin is a genealogical history that, in its unfolding, reveals the existential truth of what emerges in it. Thus, neither the self-creating of a personal God nor the innocent origin of an emerging person can be seen as metaphysical causes or events; they are far more important, fundamental, and true than any causal account. Indeed, any wisdom achieved by the unfolding of a story that reveals existential meaning is both more true and more real than any account relying on causes or presupposed entities that initiate causal series. Etiology is always inferior to history. If the history be genealogical, it assumes the quality of a fundamental understanding.

Chapter 6
Genealogy

To read Nietzsche philosophically is to endure a most frustrating anguish. Never is love conjoined with hate for what is merely read so intensely felt. In part this is due to Nietzsche's ambivalent language; he uses prose as if it were poetry, an unhealthy marriage teeming with divorce. To the flippant, such mingling is entirely acceptable, even delightful, but this acceptance merely reflects the flippancy. Prose matters as prose and poetry matters as poetry. From both truth can be learned, both can and do compliment each other, both are necessary for our existential survival. But to confuse them is to obfuscate; indeed to mingle the oil of poetry with the water of prose not only vexes the mind, it addles the spirit. The poetic stuns and reveals, charms and provokes; prose guides and refines, informs and corrects. What can a philosopher do with an aphorism? Criticize it? Deny it? Affirm it? How do you *argue* with Nietzsche? One does not argue with Shakespeare. We can, after the performance and in the tranquility of reflection, disassociate ourselves from what the poet seems to support; but in the enjoyment of his plays we suspend such critique in order to be moved. But when a powerful aphorism moves us, as if it were poetry, are we not guilty of insensitivity or pettiness if we analyze with picayune detail the content and reasoning or lack of it? Yet, if we accept it as a part of philosophy, are we not required to demand its justification and legitimacy?

The very dubiety of this incestuous coupling of the language twins undoubtedly is part of its scintillating charm. Perhaps only the rigid Fricka would censure the incest between Siegmund and Sieglinde as long as Wagner's music is playing. But to make serious moral judgments while under the intoxicant of such overwhelming music is sheer folly. While the Walsung twins are singing we cannot help but want them to succeed in their love-making. That Wagner himself recognizes the legitimacy of Fricka's censure is often overlooked even after the music stops. Incest is still incest, and to couple prose and poetry with passionate intimacy cannot be condoned.

This is not a mere petulance. It is a serious flaw, albeit a flaw that, like the Walsungs' love, reveals much that may be unreachable any other way.

It is not merely the language incest of mating prose to poetry, however, that irks the truth-hungry reader of Nietzsche. Much of what he says is simply wrong, some of it downright silly. Yet these flaws are so intertwined with legitimate and valid insight we fear tearing out the crop with the weeds. To take his works seriously as philosophy requires critique; knowing the cunning of his tactics of obfuscation is therefore a requirement for learning from him. Fortunately in this section we are concerned solely with his understanding of the meaning and origin of morals and evil. There is much to learn from him on this theme; there is also much to criticize and even reject.

In 1886 Nietzsche published *Beyond Good and Evil* (hereafter BGE); a year later be published *On a Genealogy of Morals*, (*OGM*). The latter book may seem, in some ways, an advance on the former; but both belong together. The title of the 1886 volume is used as a foil for this inquiry. Nietzsche talks about going "beyond" (Jenseits) or "that side", whereas the title of our present inquiry resists the danger of such license, and speaks of "this side" of evil. Herein, however, is one of the sources of frustration: what does Nietzsche mean by *beyond*, especially in the context of morality and evil? There are many possible understandings to the term *beyond* and unfortunately Nietzsche, as do most poets but few good philosophers, plays the term as a chord, plucking almost every string on the lexicographer's harp. The most obvious reading is something like this: not limited to. . . . Thus we might say that friendship goes "beyond" mutual advantage, meaning there is more to friendship than mere utilitarian acquaintance. There is, however, a more serious meaning, to wit: no longer controlled by . . . Thus we say the rich and powerful often can go beyond the law, or that genius goes beyond the rules. This sense of *beyond* often suggests superiority in the new realm opened up, inviting almost a disdain for what is surpassed. A third meaning to the term is a philosophical one, suggesting the transcendental, in which what is implied it the *a priori* possibility of something: that which makes something possible. The principle of cause and effect makes possible empirical science and is hence considered "beyond" (i.e., supportive of but not dependent on) science. To go beyond good and evil, then, would simply mean to step back from them and ask what they mean.

In Aphorism #153 of *BGE*, Nietzsche writes: "What is done out of love happens beyond good and evil." (Cowan translation) What does this mean? It could mean that all acts that are done because of love cannot or should not be censured at all. This would be a tawdry saying. Men have killed their rivals for love, abandoned their families for love, fought wars for it, lied for it, enslaved their beloveds, and even destroyed themselves and their beloveds out of love. To condone all such wretchedness strains our credulity. Perhaps, then, this is not what is meant. The aphorism could also mean simply that love is not the product of morality; there can be no law or algorithm to explain or justify Juliet loving Romeo, even though the Capulets would have, and subsequently did, forbid her to do so. But if this is all that is meant, none who ever loved would protest it. It is so common a piece of wisdom few would find it anything but trite. Perhaps however, we should read the aphorism this way: good and evil themselves presuppose the more fundamental reality of love. A christian might say this about the moral law coming from a loving father-god. Or an existential thinker may argue that being able to love must be presupposed if there is good and evil at all. The aphorism would then rank the existential "beyond" the moral, not in the sense of a license permitting anything, but as ranking what it means to exist as lovers as the ground and possibility of morality.

There is yet another meaning. Perhaps by the title, 'beyond good and evil' is simply meant "thinking about good and evil." That is, the enterprise is a critique, and the interesting question is now raised: how is it possible to consider what these terms mean without begging the question in some way? This suggestion gains no little support when we consider the title of his next book, for a genealogy of morals seems necessarily transmoral in some sense. This would place *BGE* in the philosophically legitimate inquiry of post-Kantian methodology: granting we make moral judgments, we now ask how we can do so. Nietzsche seems to use the term *beyond* in all of these senses; and since there are inconsistencies in the manifold of such uses, this imprecision contributes hugely to the very obfuscation he seems at times to celebrate. Unfortunately, what seems to appeal to most readers is the licentious first suggestion, especially to *fin de siècle* European artists and contemporary sophomores. It is as if Nietzsche were on a par with Oscar Wilde, George B. Shaw, and Karl Marx, criticizing 'middle class morality' with such aplomb that all morality is brought into question. It was not that long ago that any ethical restraint on any human endeavor save supporting revolutions could be dismissed with the contemptuous label, "bourgeois". This still has a chilling effect on those seeking to instill moral responsibility in an age of wanton disregard for decency and respect.

Nietzsche at times may seem to endorse this kind of nihilistic non-restraint. But, in *OGM* he cunningly remarks that whereas he was quite willing to publish a book entitled *Beyond Good and Evil* he would never have written a book entitled *Beyond Good and Bad*. This single remark is deeply troubling.

Nietzsche, apparently, is willing to go beyond good and evil but not to go beyond good and bad. The latter pair has legitimate authority, the former illegitimate. Readers of *OGM* know exactly why he says this. 'Bad' is simply that which is unworthy of a noble soul; evil is that external power which victimizes by its superiority, and hence is the whine of the ignoble. Were this true, evil should indeed be surpassed, for it would be that before which the weak hunker in cowardly fear. This strikes us as such a worthwhile discovery, uncovering an irresistible existential truth, that the support and analysis of it deserves deep appreciation. There are three points that make Nietzsche's analysis worthy of thought. The first is that an existential mode of existence—in this case, the joy in our own superiority as a way of being—is the origin of legitimate morality. The second is that morality can be understood in terms of an existential genealogy. That is, we understand what it means to be good—and hence what we ought to do—only if we see that the difference between good and bad has its origin in the pathos of superiority and our own belonging. If who I am *matters*, then, I should act in accordance with the nobility inherent in this superiority. The third is that fearsome victimhood is ignoble.

Why do these ideas attract? To take the third point first: there is a tendency in any staid and unchallenged ethos to equate goodness with weakness, or at least with untroubled passivity. It irritates a spirited soul to reduce everything to the lowest common denominator, and it further gags such a soul to find virtue in cowardice. We are aware that those who deny their own responsibility by whining about external forces that "made" them do wrong things are entirely repugnant. For them, evil is Other, like a Satan with forbidden fruit. Particularly in ages of dandified sensitivities that daintily recoil before the classic virtues such as courage, piety, loyalty and reverence toward truth, and invert them into the vices of putative vulgarity, it is refreshing to confront the bold exposé of their existential ground. When cowardice is seen as virtue and courage as vice then we must, if we matter at all, "go beyond" such nihilism. At the very least this account reveals Nietzsche's own ranking of the virtues: humility, evenhandedness, meekness, kindness and egalitarianism either rank at the bottom of the list, or are actual vices usurping the name of virtue by the ignoble victims; daring, audacity, courage, self-respect, honor, integrity, loyalty and triumph are the cardinal virtues here; and the very list sends a tingle of excitement down the back of every romantic, every social misfit, every earnest critic. Nietzsche quite rightly points out that if we distinguish the moral negatives between evil and bad we thereby also distinguish the moral positives. The term 'good' now has two distinct meanings: for the noble it means strong, for the base it means weak. As a consequence, for the noble there really is no such thing as evil; the only options for the superior person are good and bad, just as the only options for the weak are good—which now means accepting the slavery of fear—and evil.

For Nietzsche the truth of these evaluations lies in the illuminative power of what he calls "genealogy". The origin of good, evil, and bad comes from the realization of class superiority, an almost Thrasymachean trust in power, or the will to it, as the explanation of all things. With the huge energy of his language, Nietzsche batters down the defenses of altruistic self-deceit, thereby befitting his own apparent metaphysics. If the Will to Power is the fundamental reality, then only powerful language will prevail, and what the power of his language reveals is, not unexpectedly, the goodness of power and hence the badness of weakness. The self-assurance of the blonde beast is the genealogical origin of two distinct moralities: the noble's equation of power with good and the victim's equation of fearsome submission with good. Already in *BGE*, Nietzsche distinguishes the two moralities, slave and master, but now, in *OGM*, he grounds this distinction in philosophical genealogy, reducing the ethical language to the more fundamental language of metaphysics.

But is it true? What is the argumentative power of any speculative genealogy? Is it possible that some legitimate insights are here paid in far too dear a coin? The exposé of the pusillanimity of contemporary ethical prejudice may have validity, inspired by the poetic power of a great writer, but in seeking the origin of morality we also expect, nay demand, a great thinker, and though Nietzsche is surely the former it is not so obvious that here, at least, he is among the latter. Criticize we must, even if our lance is nothing but the love of truth and the dragon is a cultural behemoth. The point is not to show Nietzsche is wrong in every way but simply that he might be wrong in some way.

The context of this present inquiry provides what may seem a very small prick indeed on the leathern skin of this roaring, blonde, beast. Apparently it is ignoble to recognize the reality of evil, for such recognition debases us by inflating what is merely bad into the grotesque, overblown balloon of the evil Other. But is this declension inevitable? It is noted above that vast ideological terror can be real indeed, as when we speak of the "spread" of Naziism or Bolshevism. Since these forces are very real and very threatening, they constitute a serious assault on our own worth. We must resist them, but there is no guarantee our efforts will succeed. They are also Other; they come from without. Nietzsche seems to suggest that such dangers are not evil but bad; yet in recognizing them as Other and threatening, they are evil and hence, apparently, unworthy of our fear. This seems distortive. Why not call these forces evil, yet retain our own integrity? Why not, indeed, fear them? There is no possibility of true courage without fear; and if courage be a virtue of the noble, then fear must also be a possible characteristic. Indeed the fear is, in this instance, a great fear of what is Other. To confront this as evil seems far nobler than merely to dismiss it as unworthy of our clan. Such dismissal is self-deceit if the threat truly is dire.

If by "Other" we mean some transcendent reality that threatens beyond our ken, instilling a great sense of doom and foreboding, why should this ignoble us? Is not this precisely what Hamlet confronts? A transcendent being, a ghost from the beyond, tells the young prince to avenge a double sacrilege. How would any noble or thoughtful person react to this? Humans can perhaps avenge ordinary wrongs, (what is bad), but only the divine can avenge a sacrilege, evil. We would wonder as he does whether the vision were real; and if we discover evidence that the message at least, is true, we would still hesitate, for as human we must take responsibility for what we do, but as divinely instructed to avenge evil we seem to cede our very humanity. It takes Hamlet a while to confront this honestly, and once he sees the honor of Fortinbras' army finding nobility not in the act but in the mode of confronting it, he is transformed. Is not Nietzsche's distinction an impediment to understanding Hamlet? If evil cannot be other for a noble soul, then Hamlet is impossible. (Given the choice, I'll take *Hamlet*.)

These minor but irritating reflections provoke more serious probing. What is a genealogy of morals? Is it an attempt to explain morality by non-moral language? Does the mere historical fact that some men are stronger and more beautiful, and others are ugly and weak, explain what ought to be? Indeed, should we not be suspect of any reduction of moral understanding to *any* non-moral account? Nietzsche himself rejects certain genealogies as requiring a species of forgetting that seems to him impossible. "How is such forgetting possible?" he asks. But any and all non-moral accounts of morality entail a forgetting; and since Nietzsche seeks to give a similarly non-moral account, how is *his* forgetting possible? Furthermore, a genealogy is more than a speculative account of *origin*, for as we have seen, the beginning is not the story. Is Nietzsche claiming that because morality *begins* in the superiority of the blonde beast, it therefore must *still* be this superiority? How do we move from the beginning to any real moral judgment? Actually, the three-fold genealogy from nihilistic hedonism to nay-saying asceticism to yea-saying aestheticism in *BGE* is far more illuminating than the origin of morality sketched in *OGM*, for at least in the earlier book Nietzsche shows an impressive emergence or even historical dialectic that can appeal to a critical mind. He seems much more willing to find considerable validity in the ascetic in the earlier work.

It is to be doubted that Nietzsche uses the term *evil* in the same sense in both books. If by *evil* in *BGE* Nietzsche means the ignobly feared Other, then where is the power in claiming love is beyond it? *Anything* worthwhile is beyond it. All the power in the term *beyond* dissipates if evil be taken in the sense described in *OGM*. Nothing debases quite as effectively as debasing your opponent. If Nietzsche means by evil the awesome Other before which only slaves cower, then going beyond good and evil is merely the rejection of ordinary cowardice, and is no great achievement. All except the most craven are already "beyond" *this* sense of evil. But surely "beyond good and evil" means more than overcoming cowardice.

What seems so dubious in the later work is the inherent reductionism. Morality is "reduced" to non-moral qualities such as the feelings of importance for the "noble" blonde beast; this origin in turn is reduced to the will to power, about which Nietzsche himself seems ambivalent. He argues, for example, that the putative love of truth is "really" only a love of the will to power, as if this is to demote any worth to truth-seeking in itself. The dangers here are great. Morality ceases to be interesting if it is reduced to something else. When Freud reduces all to the sexual impulse, or Marx reduces all to the class struggle, or Hitler to race, or the mechanists to machines, one must question the reason for such reductions. In all of them both the reality and the truth of moral and ethical judgments are denied. Rather than being the genealogy of morals, Nietzsche's reduction becomes the castration of morals.

This reading is admittedly only one part or facet of what Nietzsche seems to say. Especially in *BGE* he seems to retain the autonomous— i.e., non-reductionist—status to morality. But the lure of metaphysics is especially strong in *OGM*, and with this lure, the proliferation of the sophistic shibboleth "really" almost strangles the passion to truth altogether. Morality is "really" the arrogant hegemony of the blonde beast; moral thinking is "really" only a stage in the unfolding of the genealogy; the superiority of the blonde beast is "really" only the will to power. The will-to-power is "really" a mere description of the world as it is, and unless the reader accepts this he "really" is nothing but a slave-moralist. All obedience is "really" out of fear, all punishment is "really" revenge. Armed with this remarkable term, a veritable prolixity of theories abound: the world is "really" water, love is "really" lust, persons are "really" machines. Allowing this term as a reductionist weapon to anyone who seeks to avoid confronting hard issues is an insidious species of egalitarian thinking inconsistent with Nietzsche's finer instincts.

Nietzsche does not avoid the hard questions; his flamboyant style merely masks a genuine though flawed contribution. It is imperative to ask what a genealogical account means, and why such an account may be necessary, particularly for such notions as evil and morality. What, in the original sense, was so important about genealogy? The political purpose in a primogenitive Europe was to establish the *legitimacy* of sovereignty. The arguments in Shakespeare's *Henry V* show the importance of this. If the king could not establish, through genealogical research, the origin of his claim, then his assumption of the throne would be merely the imposition of sheer power, power without authority, and thus invite any subsequent claimant to use the same brutal means. There were often rather dubious contortions, of course, as well as genuine contenders with seemingly equal persuasion; but there can be no doubt that in the political history of the west, legitimacy mattered, however connived; and with this demand for legitimacy the need for genealogies became imperative. Show me your lineage, and if a sufficient amount of royal blood flows in your veins, your claim to the throne or the family inheritance is not a mere usurpation of sheer power.

Genealogy therefore, seeks to find both in the origin and descent of families, a justification of legitimacy. The question at hand is the justification and legitimacy of morality and evil. Are they merely usurpers—that is: notions that have crept in unawares without legitimacy—or are they truly justified notions that, on the basis of their genealogical origins, legitimately belong in our understanding? And if they are legitimate, what rank do they have? Are they merely baronic, or ducal, or are they regal?

What are the resources of a philosophical genealogy? There are no birth certificates, no genealogical courts passing down judgments, no memories that stretch back with any authority to the conceptual beginning. Are we then left with mere fantasies? Stories made up out of the thinker's rich imagination? Or can the off-spring be identified with tell-tale characteristics of inheritance: the long, patrician nose of the Hapsburgs, the red hair of the Tudors, the flabby faces of the Hohenzollerns? Why is one genealogy better than another?

The very fact of genealogy shows the vulnerability of the claims. There were no need to do a genealogy of morals were the authority of such imperatives not questionable in two dire ways. The first is the very legitimacy of morality itself. Perhaps there are no morals. At best they are merely customs, at worst idle stories that induce fear, restricting our freedom. The second is perhaps less draconian but more vexing: given the different genealogies, there are different claimants, and what morality means is altered profoundly by the story selected to ground its legitimacy. How the origin and history unfolds would then determine to some meaningful extent what we ought to do. As a consequence, the superiority of one genealogy over the other is of capital and urgent importance. But how is such superiority gauged?

We first note the negatives. Genealogies cannot be natural histories. There is, after all, *no* physical evidence for any natural history of morals. Speculative leaps into our pre-literate origins always beg the question. It *may be* that at one time the weaker members of a loosely organized tribe obeyed the strongest member simply out of fear; but we can never know this. Even if we assume it, it is not in itself sufficient to account for how we think about morality now. One speculative account of natural history is just as valid as another, which is to say no speculative account is legitimate at all. To say primitive people were not yet sophisticated enough to distinguish fear from reverence or respect also begs the questions. How do we know this? How could we possibly know it? Furthermore, whatever else a genealogy of morals might be, it simply cannot be a causal account, in which non-moral beliefs or attitudes "somehow" get translated over long periods into moral judgments, for the vagueness of the "somehow" is always the weakest link, and to leave that link untested in again to beg the question. Kant is quite right in this: one cannot derive the "ought" from the "is".

If genealogies are not natural histories, nor series of sociological causes, then how are they possible? Only if they represent an existential uncovering of what it means to be moral can they provide the necessary legitimacy of the inheritance. The analogy here with inherited traits is now of considerable importance. If the queen's paramour is blue-eyed and blonde, and her husband the king is swarthy and brown-eyed, the suspect child's blue-eyed blondness may raise serious questions of his paternity. Unless the inherited traits of the descendent are found in the genealogical origins of the progenitors the account may be misleading or false, putting a bastard on the throne. We cannot know directly when the first moral judgment was made, nor what brought it about, so any metaphysical appeal is entirely speculative and ultimately worthless. But we do, right now in the present, already have moral judgments, and we can now ask what it means to have them, and part (though not all) of what this possession means may be illuminated by a genealogical sketch that remains true to the inherited stamp. We do not speak here of specific moral claims. We do not, in other words, accept the claim that murder is wrong and then go backward in time showing that the putative origin of such a claim lies in the ability to imagine ourselves as victims, and hence argue that fear of death is the genealogical source of our proscription against homicide. Rather, we ask: what does it mean to be moral at all, and then consider what existential modalities must be assumed, given who we are now and what we know of our own historical becoming.

If we ask the question in this way, Nietzsche's contribution is impressive. Morality properly conceived is superiority—indeed it is self-conscious superiority. A fundamental characteristic of this superiority is its rejection of baseness or slavery. A slave—even in the case of being a slave to one's own meaner instincts—cannot be free; and as not free, is not superior. The slave is weak in the most wretched sense of the word: an adopted or even chosen weakness, a weakness embraced as a species of cowering inferiority. This weakness of slavery, when pressed, requires a pseudo-morality which consists solely of fearsome obedience to a master's commands, all the more degrading in that these imperatives have no other justification than that they are the arbitrary commands of the noble, powerful master. This genealogy rings true precisely because *all* the elements of its descriptive power are still with us, present in every human soul as it struggles with itself.

That every one of these descriptive elements has been defended by prior philosophers need not detract. The ancient Greeks, especially Plato, and the Romans would have recognized the truth of them, for they had long ago realized that what really matters in ethics is that moral conduct leads to a better existence. But it is not just the ancients; even Kant recognizes that human worth lies not in the avoidance of, but the acceptance of, responsibility. Indeed, even Nietzsche's seeming opponents, the christians, have among them many who argue in the same way, as do Scotus and Augustine. It is important to realize that Nietzsche's master-morality is not lacking in laws, as if the noble are free to do what they want. (To be free to do what one *wants*, of course, is to be a slave to our desires, and not really free at all. Nietzsche realizes this.) It is rather that what a law means is different to a master than to a slave.

The isolation of the slave-moralist as distinct from master-moralist grounds the next important distinction: evil is not the same as bad. That there must be such a distinction is not here denied. Indeed Nietzsche's original insight still holds: we must distinguish evil from bad just because the existential is distinct from the moral, so that the worth in the former is distinct from, and possibly the ground of, the worth in the latter. Who we are matters independently of and prior to what we do. It is the phrase 'and prior to' that gives the singularly *genealogical* authority to Nietzsche's account. By telling the story in this way—that is, by unfolding the truth from its fundamental origin—Nietzsche provides a philosophical method for making the existentially significant truth of our own meaning capable of reflection. We can now *think*, and not merely opine, about what it means to be—as moral.

It is precisely the greatness of this contribution, a contribution which has some precedents, to be sure, that weakens his critique of evil. For if existential worth is distinct, and perhaps even more fundamental than, moral worth, then we must be prepared to reflect on what it means to succeed and fail as existentially worthy. We must, in other words, recognize that evil is, exactly as Nietzsche says, the threat of the Other; but not only as external other before whose lash we must always submit, but as *becoming* Other, i.e., *losing* our existential worth. Unless it is possible to fail on this level, the level itself is meaningless. Nobility is not a sinecure. If slavery and its inherent baseness can be either self-induced, as when we become slaves to our own lusts, or other-induced, when we capitulate to the raw power of externalist threat, then nobility can be threatened either by internal diminishment or by capitulation to external influences. In both cases it is the internal rot that disturbs most. Since this danger threatens our autonomy or even integrity, leading us to become other than ourselves because we are governed by forces that are not our own, it must be called evil, even by the terminological standards of Nietzsche's description. What is bad is still unworthy of us, and what is evil is still the threat of Otherness. Nietzsche, to complete his genealogy, accounts for Otherness as the triumphant conquest of the noble over the base, so that only the slaves fear, and indeed hate, that which is greater than they. But it seems there can be a legitimate fear of *becoming* other, even for the noble.

There is another point to be made about genealogies. If their primary purpose it to establish legitimacy, this can be done not only by showing the right of an heir, but also to show how the heritage itself is thinkable. Even if there were no quarrels about what is right and wrong, even if we all shared a common understanding of the funda-

mental principles, as philosophers we still would want to know what
it means to be moral at all, and to be evil at all, and an existential
genealogy might well show us how to think in this way. Since this
present labor is concerned less with the first and more with the second of these questions, we can raise the problem in this way: what
does it mean, in terms of origins and genealogies, to confront evil?
Nietzsche's answers seems to be: cowardly weakness, rooted in the
fear of original superiority and strength. This in turn seems to imply
that to confront evil at all is already to manifest a slave's mentality,
since the noble confront only what is bad. If, however, the origin of
evil is seen not in the fearsome but in the fundamental nature of
reality, an entirely different genealogy emerges. Our origin is thus
innocence, which, while providing the continuing heritage of being
precious simply because of who we are, is necessarily shown as a lacking, and hence always as a beginning that, though remembered, must
be overcome in the acceptance of our responsibility. Evil is therefore
not the result of mere fear, judgment, or even condemnation, but is
real, depending on and yet also establishing the reality of our ourselves as persons. This unguilty origin persists, as an aching realization of one-time purity, which mocks our fall from grace even as it is
supplanted by a greater mode existence that cannot nor would not
return, since responsibility matters. Only because evil is real can the
judgments of morality find legitimacy in the inheritance to which
we are blinded in original innocence. Evil is real; moral acts can sequester and thwart the hegemony of the reality, only because goodness in the sense of existential worth (nobility—not innocence) is
also real.

Regardless of how we account for such genealogies there is always a
danger inherent in such thinking. There is what might be called 'the
paradox of depth,' vaguely akin to the paradox of analysis. The deeper
we dig, the further we abandon the felt immediacy of the problem
itself. We may plunge so deep that we sink, or even drown, in the
attempt to explain, especially if the explanations are reductionistic,
or if, as is more frequent, the explanations themselves become more
fuliginous than the problem. It is a phenomenon all too familiar
among the academics; we become so fascinated with the heady va-
pors of the deep that they begin to take on an allure of their own, an
intoxicant of putative profundity that beguiles the clever. It may never
occur to us that reflections on both the "origins" and "genealogies" of

good, bad, and evil may derail the reason we probe in the first place. Perhaps there is no genealogy of morals. Would we, for example, undertake a genealogy of pleasure? Surely pleasure is so immediate and so fundamental that no non-pleasurist account could possibly reveal to us anything we do not already understand; indeed, a genealogy of pleasure may be toxic to the healthy grasp of what it means. The greatest insult to a hedonistic ethics is not that some pleasures may be immoral, but that to burden the joyous acceptance of our delights with the dreadful yoke of the 'ought' suffocates all life out of what is wonderful on its own. You mean I *ought* to smell this rose? I *ought* to enjoy the sweetness of its odor? That I am somehow morally deficient if I do not take pleasure in smelling it? This is the tyranny of the Ought, enslaving all feeling under the hegemony of grim morality. Pleasure pleases, and part of its pleasing is simply because there is no further need to explain it whatsoever. Perhaps morality and evil are like pleasure: they need no genealogy to justify them, and any attempt to provide one is treacherous.

Perhaps, however, there is a legitimate genealogy of pleasure, in spite of the caveat just described. Certainly we can rank pleasures, and just as certainly we can add to the pleasure of pleasures by thinking about it. But the caveat still holds. It does not indict all genealogies, but warns us that the genealogy cannot usurp the reality, any more than the vita cannot usurp the life.

It is this reason that explains the title of the present work. We are in danger of going so far "beyond" good and evil that we lose sight of them altogether. Nietzsche himself rejects those genealogies that require a forgetting that strains our credulity. It is a strain on this credulity that reduces the confrontation with evil to mere cowardice before a magnificent power. Let us assume Nietzsche is correct, and then go one more step "beyond" his account. For us, the now ennobled readers, evil is nothing but *mistake*. We ought not, if we are to be true to what is noble in us, admit the validity of the notion altogether. We accept the bad, but evil is a chimera, feared only by the base. It does not, for us truth-seekers, really exist. We have lost a term. Is this a nobler existence? Or does it merely make us feel better to believe it? What we want to know is whether this erasure of a term from the legitimate text of our language is justified. Do we test its veracity by going one step further, deeper, more profoundly *beyond*?

Or must we not finally admit, that, what ever we mean by a genealogy or by stepping beyond, we must ultimately return to *this* side of evil? This, at least, should be obvious: any genealogy that bars us from returning to the original confrontation—bars us, that is, from coming back to this side of evil—is highly suspect. For it is precisely on this side of evil that we dwell.

If we must, as philosophers go deeper, even as we accept the caveat inherent in the paradox of depth, how should we proceed? We seek to understand evil. Are genealogies and origins the only, or even best, ways to go "deeper" than our ordinary understandings of the phenomenon? Perhaps what is lacking in our inheritance of the problem is not depth so much as breadth. Evil, as a phenomenon, is ubiquitous and has many guises. It is a species of narrow-mindedness to approach so fecund and fundamental a notion solely in terms if its origins. If evil be a part of us, and if we seem to learn about ourselves often in terms of the cultural sacraments known as artworks that mirror who we are, perhaps a further attempt to achieve a deeper understanding of evil is to see it reflected in the looking-glass of culture.

Chapter 7
Mirrored Evil

Iago stuns. If the performance be at all inspired, the naked evil of Othello's trusted servant moves us uncomfortably and deeply. We leave the theatre hounded by devils, devastated by the collapse of a nobly inspired general, apparent victim of singular cunning and the absolute banality of a dropped handkerchief. If Iago be not evil, no one deserves the ignominy of that censure: he seems the paradigm. What is the character of this man that, in our dramatic revealing, we find so fascinating?

When examined critically, relying on the actual text, we are, however, entirely disappointed. For it develops that Iago is rather inept, not very exciting; and most disturbing of all, he is shallow. How can this be? The dramaturgic thrill of this wonderfully sketched character seems, in the artform, to checkmate the philosophical gambit of Kant, Nietzsche and Arendt who clepe evil banal. But the tragic loss in this play is not banal; it is monstrous. What is trite about the slippery feints and prodigious will of this thoroughly despicable yet riveting man? In the first act we hear him tell Roderigo that he hates the moor; he then gives two reasons, one publicly, the other privately in soliloquy: he is bitter at having been passed over for promotion, and he wonders if he is cuckold by his general. There is no evidence given us to support the latter claim, nor does Iago make any attempt to verify it. Given the characters of both his wife and Othello, there is nothing to suggest it is true and much to suggest it is false; but Iago believes it, or *pretends* to believe it to fan his hate. What do these admissions tell us about him? Though it always stings when we are passed over for a promotion, unless Othello is grossly deficient in one of the most important roles of a general—deciding whom to promote—there must have been a sound reason. We are told in a host of ways that Othello is not only a good general but a great one; since wise promoting is essential for a successful army, we must assume Othello's judgment is well-grounded. We are also told, almost to satiety, that Othello finds Iago to be trust-worthy. What we seem to have, therefore, is the picture of a faithful, trusted servant who has long been appreciated because of his honesty, and who, in spite of this, and in spite of the support of three politicians, is passed over for

Michael Cassio. The nature of this honesty is the key. There is no reason to accuse Othello of gross misjudgment in matters military: Iago has been honest—as a good, time-tested clerk or private secretary is honest. The years of his dutiful if unspectacular performance inspire a picture of a valet or aide or even a competent corporal, reliable in the daily skills of filling out forms and familiar with logistical bureaucracy. He is thus a small-minded bureaucrat: neat, precise, efficient, and possible afflicted with the paranoia of such types. In short he is exactly as he describes Cassio. (Cassio cannot be as Iago sees him, since later in the play he replaces Othello as governor of Cyprus by judgment of the Venetian Senate.)

Perhaps his hatred for Othello is suddenly and newly felt; or it may have been simmering for a long time beneath the surface and just now, by the promotions, fully realized. In either case it has been carefully muted, a sure guarantee that it quickly will become a passion. We know in the first hundred lines that, outside of his clerkish duty, he is not honest at all, for he has been taking gross advantage of the piteous Roderigo. He is, then, a cheap thief, a would-be pimp, a manipulator of the stupid, cruel to those beneath him, totally vulgar (only Iago could describe the act of love as the beast with two backs), yet obsequious to the mighty. And he hates himself even as he deceives himself into thinking he loves himself.

But we say, he is profoundly cunning. Is he? Actually by his own admission his plans have put him in a most parlous state. If either Roderigo or Cassio or Bianca or even Amelia is not silenced either by terror or death, Iago is doomed. This is not at all a well-designed campaign. Indeed, it is hardly a campaign at all; it is more a series of half-baked reactions to opportunities. He does not even look ahead with ordinary prudence; indeed there is no evidence that he ever has a real plan; he is gleeful at the successes that sheer fortuity brings, not of what his so-called cunning brings. He does however, possess that instinct for the weakness of others that almost all sullen people have; but this is due not to any superiority of their wit but simply because, aching to hurt others, their meanness gives them cruel eyes.

He does, though, seem to be able to lead Othello to distraction. Is this, at least, not masterful? It is perhaps adept, perhaps even artful, but his victory is due far more to the inner anguish of Othello himself than to any brilliance on Iago's part. We need not be churlish here; Iago is clever in provoking Othello's jealousy, but most of his success even here is due to his meanness: anyone who takes such personal glee in hurting others will use methods and techniques that, being amoral, are unexpected among the decent, and hence are liable to succeed. The more we mark the passage of his cunning, the more flawed it is; it advances more by the vulnerability of his victims than by any brilliance on his part, save in his deceit. But the deceit is possible only because of Othello's warrior trust. It is indeed the warrior's trust in another warrior, coupled with the strange but wonderful leadership of Othello and his enormous piety to all oaths, particularly the martial and the marital, that deserves our fascination with this tragic decline.

It is not the greatness of Iago that makes his being evil so formidable, but the greatness of the evil that makes Iago formidable. Evil people are almost always banal; but evil itself must, perforce, be "great," precisely in the prodigy of its astonishment. It is perhaps obvious that those with great gifts can do much good as well as much harm, but this does not mean that there is greatness in the evil man. Since evil threatens the very existential worth of our reality, it itself can be no banality, any more than the physical health of our bodies can accept cancer as banal. It is therefore not merely in Iago's character that the play succeeds in its power to reveal evil.

Among the many villains in Shakespeare's plays Iago stands out. Richard III, Skylock, Macbeth, Claudius, Malvolio and Don Pedro are all terrific personalities with their full accommodations of malice, but they have other qualities to make them fascinating. Iago, unlike them, seems singularly bereft of any quality save petty hatred. For, remove this hatred from him, and what is interesting about him? The closet approximations to him may be Goneril and Regan, for they too seem to resent being passed over in affection by their father's preference for Cordelia, and respond by amoral, icy revenge and the cruelty of ingratitude. All three are greatly evil; none are great and evil. (Richard III and Macbeth may be both great and evil; yet they do not fascinate us as paradigmatically evil as does Iago and to a lesser extent, Lear's pelican daughters.) Perhaps what spots Iago is precisely this: that, were his villainy removed, nothing would be left over. This may explain why, after his arrest, he simply refuses ever to speak again. Quite literally, he has nothing more to say since there is nothing more to him. His shallowness is paraded blatantly; consider his advice to Roderigo: live for the moment, take nothing seriously, put money in thy purse, win Iago's admiration by becoming coldly selfish, seek to understand the vulnerability of others solely for the sake of manipulating personal gain. The more Iago succeeds in molding the soft and fetid cheese of Roderigo's soul to be like himself, the more he despises this rich, spoiled brat, and hence himself. Roderigo becomes a vile mirror to Iago's own soul, dramatically revealing the self-loathing that is the heart of Iago's entire existence. Shakespeare rarely wastes a character, and Roderigo is a disgusting but profoundly important member of the *dramatic personae*. For this foppish fluff has Iago as his mentor and abuser, and the student reflects the teacher. Even in this reflection, however, Iago pales: Roderigo at least has the raw gumption to assault Cassio twice; Iago is too cowardly to fight any unwounded man directly, though sheer fear and hatred compels him to stab to death his own wife lest she reveal the damning truth.

These indictments show the pettiness and even stupidity of Iago, not his putative brilliance in cunning. He does know how to stir the latent jealousy of Othello because he himself is jealous even if falsely. Yet, the sheer evil that emanates putridly from this vile wretch nevertheless overwhelms us with its significance. That it overwhelms is a truth that demands our respect.

To grasp the nature of this evil as parallel with the tawdry fortuity in the drama is revealing. It seems almost demeaning that so much should hang upon so trivial a misfortune as dropping a handkerchief. This is almost comically absurd—that a great man should be destroyed by so petty a slip. Surely Shakespeare could have invented a somewhat less childish misdemeanor, something worthy of our attention. Of course it is precisely the insignificance of the event that his genius sports as compelling, for the sheer banality of it forces us to wonder at it. Iago is exactly like the handkerchief: utterly trite, yet the catalyst of total devastation. The point is not the Thomas Hardy-like focus on the mundane; it is rather the wedding of fate and freedom together in such integrated wholeness that we realize being fated is necessary to being free and that fate requires freedom. The more we seek to find a message of human impotence in the face of coincidence, the more we are misled; the more we seek to find a causally sufficient motive in the crude cunning of Iago, the more we avoid the play itself. Indeed, the more we seek to interpret tragedy as some morally deserved fall of a great hero, the further we stray from its genius. The point is: the existential greatness of Othello persists even with his moral collapse. Drama must find its essence in the audience, not on the stage; and for us in the audience what is so mighty is the induced realization that Othello's worth is not eclipsed by his dreadful loss nor the supreme folly of his misjudgment. His success is sacrificied to let his meaning shine through. Not even the greatest misfortunes entirely corrupt his magnificence. Othello fails, but his greatness persists—without this, tragedy would not appeal. Iago lacks anything of existential worth; and thus he reveals evil.

It is Othello, after all who kills Desdemona, not Iago. Yet this great sacrilege does not seem to mark the general as evil. Iago merely seeks to torment his victim with psychological manipulations—a petty meanness—yet he is an agent of evil. One of the most excruciating lines among so many excruciating lines is Othello's reprimand of Desdemona's identifying what he intends as murder; he calls it sacrifice. This is almost too painful to hear. Can he really see it as a sacrifice, to some God or Principle? Sacrifice is a warrior's word. We are watching poor Desdemona plea for her innocent life, and the ligatures of justice seem to strangle our hearts as we long achingly for her to escape, yet the vast denuding of Othello's mind here overtakes us briefly: he truly thinks this is a sacrifice, as the soldier offers up what is precious on the altar of battle. The folly of his judgment overwhelms more than the abuse of her innocence. We must be careful here in the refrigeration of distance: Othello is not insane; his misjudgment is criminal, his killing immoral. He would not have us excuse—'nothing extenuate'. Yet, for all this, for all the admitted immorality and justified censure, it is Iago, the nihilist, who reeks of evil, not Othello, the wrong-doer.

Othello is a curious play by Shakespeare's standards. There are no sub-plots at all, which alone makes it unique. Why? Nothing should be allowed to distract from the simple, direct unfolding of the plot and the subsequent development of the few central characters. The purity of Desdemona, the nobility of Othello, the charm of Cassio, the villainy of Iago are uncharacteristically direct and uncompromised. There is no comic relief as there usually is before the final denouement, there are no dramatic grace-notes nor unnecessary but fascinating minor characters. This is a naked play, in which the urgent, almost frenetic thrust of the plot impels us, like arrows shot from a tightly strung bow, to the grim inevitable target. The dramatic artist here senses profoundly that any distraction from the plot would flaw the sense of inevitable doom rooted in the lead characters. It is thus that Iago's naked villainy is revealed entirely without excuse or mitigation. Being noble, neither Othello nor Desdemona are quite fit to deal with such petty meanness. It is because Iago's plotting threatens the very greatness of his victims that his villainy is so monstrous and hence so evil.

These last reflections, however, require a refinement of our language. Perhaps evil is revealed only in the dramatic unfolding of the story. The fallen handkerchief, as a manifestation of fate, conjoined with the spiritual meanness of Iago's character, confronted by the noble natures of Desdemona and Othello, all combine, as elements in the overall artwork, to reveal the reality of evil. This aesthetic mirroring therefore suggests that evil is not merely in Iago's wicked will nor Othello's tragic misjudgments. Nor is it merely in the falling of a handkerchief. It is their conjunction, woven as a tapestry of fate and freedom into an enormous, tragic truth. Perhaps, then, one should not, strictly speaking, speak of Iago as evil, but as a malevolent agent of evil. This would make evil greater than any individual agent, who may indeed be banal (Pace, Arendt et.al.), but who, as elements of an unfolding plot, contribute to the cataclysmic reality of evil. We may still peak of Iago as evil, but only in a metaphoric and contributive sense. Hence the study of his character is important to our understanding of the play but cannot be seen as the sufficient cause or locus of evil.

The impact of this drama further undermines the Nietzschean suggestion that the concept of evil is fitting only for the base. Iago may be base, but the range of evil far exceeds his baseness. Othello's murder or sacrifice of his wife may be bad—i.e., immoral—but it, too, is a part of the greater evil that is the reality within this unfolding story. What makes Iago stand out among other tragic villains is the fact that almost the entire play is nothing else than his cruel, deliberate, planning of unspecific destruction, simply for the sake of evil. We watch it happen from start to finish, and the sense of impotence at unfairness is huge.

There is a paradox here. Shakespeare is far too fine a dramatist ever to create a stock, one-sided villain. He makes even the worst of men strangely sympathetic; not because he doubts their guilt or mutes our censure, but because as complex, having both strengths and weaknesses, such a character is far more interesting. This is how he presents us with Skylock, Richard III, Claudius, and the others. But with Iago the challenge is greater; for he is presented entirely without redeeming features. Only the greatest dramatist could do this: create an uninteresting man who nevertheless fascinates. By making him so banal the evil that he reveals is all the more menacing; as a consequence Iago becomes a mesmerizing power, his very pettiness a source of grisly awe. From his character we learn that it is the very banality of evil men that makes evil itself so monstrous. So brilliant is Shakespeare that, in showing us this stunning truth, we learn to turn our reflections from the vile Iago to the magnificent character of Othello, where they properly belong.

It is extremely difficult to crate in literature a pure and innocent soul who is not dull. Desdemona is a rare success. Dostoyevski's Prince Mishkin in *The Idiot* does not succeed as well as Alyosha in *The Brothers Karamozov*. Part of the reason for this is that Prince Mishkin is supposed to be the central character, with no one else his par; and this strains our acceptance of him; but Alyosha is but one of three brothers, so his innocence stands out in the broader context of this lusty family. These successes are all the more remarkable in their rarity, and they are sketched with the pens of the greatest writers. Yet, pure and innocent souls seem necessary as foils to genuine evil, and the extreme difficulty in making them interesting may be in part due to a similar difficulty in making evil emerge as a powerful reality without making it attractive. Herman Melville's much reworked masterpiece, *Billy Budd* succeeds in the creation of an almost radiant innocent, Billy, as a foil to the agency of evil imbedded in the character of the Master-at-Arms, Claggart.

Unlike Iago, Claggart is known by the other characters for his malevolence; Captain Vere retains him because he instills enough fear in the crew to establish the harsh but necessary authority on a ship of war. But Vere also waits, believing that the sheer venom in Claggart will eventually lead him to transgress the strict martial code, allowing Vere then to punish him by legitimate means. Claggart is perhaps worthier of our reflection than Iago, for there seems a real mystery: how can one as educated, so gifted, so obviously talented for higher office, be seemingly content with the demi-world of the sea's sergeants?

The curious *ambivalence* of these military roles of authority is themselves of interest. Shakespeare's "ancient" is a distortion of "ensign", which itself means a flag-bearer. Master-at-arms is akin to an army sergeant—not quite officer, not quite common soldier, never familiar with either; almost necessarily lonely because as a link between the world of command and the world of obedience they belong nowhere. It is a fitting place for evil to flourish. They are never entirely responsible, since such absolute burden is left to commanders; yet they actually are more direct in their power over others. As middle men they can hate the elite officers and disdain the common soldier or sailor. They are "officers without commission"—a curious notion in itself, as if there were a general pretense, an agreed-upon deceit. We all know that without effective sergeants there is no effective army, but history notes no great sergeant just as it notes no great teacher. By dint of office they must be remembered, if at all, only by the select few who actually work under or over them. It is almost a literary necessity that they be cynical—though in actual fact many retain loyalty as well as a love for the service. It is not incidental that both Claggart and Iago are in this strange half-world in systems where absolute power lurks behind every success.

Captain Vere notes that Billy's innocence is almost as unnatural as Claggart's evil; neither can be grasped by our ordinary understanding, yet both are understood precisely as believable characters, which is a testament to Melville's skill. Claggart's evil pre-exists Billy's arrival, but only in the confrontation itself do both innocence and evil emerge as palpable truths. There is, as with Iago, both jealousy and cruelty in Claggart; they are both in position of the sergeant's intermediate authority, they both have almost unbelievable innocents as their targets, in both cases the tragic clash is brought about by the banality of a most capricious and unlikely accident. Furthermore, in both cases the clash between the agent of evil and the radiantly innocent does not involve the central dramatic character: in spite of its title, the sea story is about Captain Vere; the Elizabethan drama is about Othello. Yet Claggart is unlike Iago because he seems to prefer his murky status of half-officer. The seeming reason for this is chilling: he does not want the full responsibility of high command even though his talents are fitting, for in this gray middle he is closer to the smell of fear and the crack of the lash. He wants the men to hate him, for their hatred, in his mind, justifies his own for them. He therefore seems a more persistent, long-time sadist, with no prior history of obsequious self-deceit. He sacrifices his superior natural gifts simply to satisfy his lust for inflicting pain, and this makes him all the more remarkable and all the more repulsive. Yet, like Iago, neither can he been excised by madness.

There are other forces at work, of course: Captain Vere's Kantian devotion to duty, the truly ugly laws that govern his majesty's ships, the tangled web of small fortuities, the awful stench of war itself looming over the waters. Evil is larger than the mere characters, and Vere, to his own dismay, realizes it. In both stories the inevitability of the plot is palpably felt, and this inevitability seems an essential part of evil. Both the agents of evil and the angels of innocence seem caught up in a whirlpool of destiny that pull them under by irresistible force. We feel this force, but do not excuse because of it. Both goodness and evil require the dialectic tension between destiny and freedom. Indeed there is no freedom without fate, nor is there any fate without freedom. Evil is not fate and goodness is not innocence: they both are rooted in the dialectical tension between the inevitable and the free. Perhaps this is why evil is real, precisely because it weds the wickedness of character with the inevitability of fate, whereas immorality is seen solely as a quality of free agents.

It is not Claggart, however, who puts Billy to death, any more than it is Iago who strangles Desdemona: that grim duty falls upon the unfortunate shoulders of Captain Vere, which is why he and not Billy is the true hero of the story. In this the dire weight of inevitability bears down on us with unwanted opprobrium. The harsh, sharp logic of the moralist presses down on us with its fatalistic inevitability; the oath that makes Vere captain screws down tightly on his judgment. The law, heinous though it be, binds them all: there is no room for grace; war permits no latitude for commander or seaman. This dour logic leads some to use the story as a crowbar to lift the heavy stone of duty and prove all who follow it alone immoral and unfree. Melville is wiser than all who criticize in this way. A warship is meaningless without duty and command. We may forget that Vere's strategy almost worked: Claggart was being crushed by the same inevitable machinery of the law that would soon crush Billy and Vere. Were it not for the dropped handkerchief of Claggart's unusually thin skull cracking against the joist, the Master at arms would have been shown an abuser of his power, and Vere would have his triumph. How do we make sense of the curious union of all these banal elements caught in the dread current of the story's plot? The force is there in the inevitability of the artwork; it is greater than any single factor, including the free wills of the moral agents. The thematic weaving by the artist's genius is not arbitrary or wanton; it is indeed a reflection of reality. This reality, greater than any of its parts, is evil itself, threading as a species of fateful power all the lines into the rope that hangs the angel, Billy. Evil is the reality that grounds these disparate events into the thrust of inevitability, dooming the innocent. Yet, this existential power is not finally triumphant. The good and decent Vere must hang the innocent boy, and the evil inherent in this, rooted in the villainy of Claggart but not limited to it, cannot deny the even greater victory visible only to us, the audience: the worth of the Captain and his unfortunate beloved sailor yet remains. This seems almost to be the cheat of art, robbing inevitability of its nihilism. But art is the mirror of reality, so if there is a cheat in the art there is likewise a cheat outside the artworks. This cheat is the inherited innocence that persists throughout our trials and losses: the existential worth that it the basis of forgiveness.

Is then the reality of evil in our actual histories akin to the reality of our destiny? Our lives are meaningful—and hence, real—as the unfolding of our stories. The narrative or dramatic thrust mirrors the temporal thrust of our own existence, and in the threaded lines of this historical uncovering the real struggle between the opposing realities of good and evil make us who we are. This suggestion is not some fanciful speculation; it is felt, powerfully, as guilt and loss are felt, in the threatre or in the pages of the novel. If evil is felt in the unfolding of a play as transcending the moral qualities in the characters, and if plays are, as Hamlet suggests, mirrors of ourselves, then there is a good reason to locate evil and its noble opposite in the reality of our own existential destinies. The artwork reveals this truth.

"It is better to rule in hell than serve in heaven." So speaks Satan in Milton's "Paradise Lost." Curiously, Milton seems at first to fail here. With lines like these we cannot but feel a deep, though troubling, sympathy. Satan is heroic in this English epic; indeed so magnificent is he that even through he is supposed to be our arch-enemy he seems rather like a defender of our deepest privacy: not even in the vaunted bliss of a new Eden can we accept slavery or even servitude, if that is all we are. Has ever a villain been more gloriously described? If this be evil, then Nietzsche smiles, and the puritan's quaking in fear of it must need be deemed unworthy. Anyone bold enough, like Satan, to take on God himself deserves admiration for his gutsy courage if nothing else.

It is not Satan who is the true hero of this epic, but Eve. Nor does Milton fail by depicting evil so greatly that it becomes a virtue. Once we realize that evil must be greatly feared, lest confronting it achieves but a cheap victory, the magnificence of Satan can be appreciated without falling into Nietzsche's trap. From *this* side of evil we still must realize the counter-argument: unless the enemy is mighty the victory over it is small. If Satan be admired for taking on the infinite power of God, so we must be admired by taking on so formidable a foe. What we must realize is that Satan fails, not only in the titanic struggle with Michael in the operatic grandeur of the opening books, where his failure is inevitable, but also with Eve, where his failure seems impossible. Indeed, in a remarkably powerful way, his failure with Eve is even more dismal than his failure with God. He leaves the latter battlefield still roaring his defiance even in defeat; from Eve he *slinks* away, not to be heard from again. God defeats Satan, but it is Eve, not God, who disgraces him.

This may seem a somewhat unorthodox reading, but only at its first sounding. Only those who deny the problem of evil fail to see the need for reverential learning from a great poet. The point need not be labored. Satan, disguised as a serpent, does indeed tempt Eve, first by lying to her (the serpent did not achieve human speech by eating of the fruit) and then by revealing a great truth, asking why it would be a sin to know. But it is not Satan's reasoning, but Eve's own thinking that convinces her. In Book Nine, from lines 750 to 780, we read Eve tempting Eve; her reasoning is far more profound than his, for she recognizes that only as free is she truly of worth, and only in knowing of good and evil is she truly free. That Milton put such deep insights into her own private, silent reflections makes her wiser than Satan, and makes her freer than Satan. She is even a better tempter than Satan. If Satan is magnificent in his refusal merely to serve in heaven, preferring to rule in hell, Eve is even more magnificent in preferring to die freely on earth than to live unfree in Eden. Satan's bombast is arrogance, Eve's quieter reflection is true pride.

Furthermore, Eve triumphs over Satan by retaining her worth in being redeemed. Her origin is innocence, and though it is an innocence necessarily lost in her gain of freedom, its inheritance carries

over in her ability to forgive and to be forgiven. The heroic spectacle
of Satan's magnificent will is necessary to show us how formidable
evil truly is; but his slinking away, defeated even in his deceit, re-
stores the greater worth of a person created in innocence but realized
in self-generated freedom.

The prodigy of Satanic evil, however, is still threatening. As an
anthropomorphized force, external to Eve and hence ourselves, this
evil is real. As real, it is distinct from Eve's own—and our own—
decision to act; yet it does not remove our responsibility even though
it lurks as an ever-present force behind it. The literary device of legitimate anthropomorphism thus shows the possibility of a distinct,
externalist evil that does not reduce us to Nietzsche's sycophants cowering before the power of this reality, striving to escape censure. We
can still be free and believe in the reality of evil. Indeed, it may be
essential for our freedom to distinguish being freely bad from being
an agent of evil. The figure of Satan as anthropomorphized evil thus
is quite distinct from the reality of evil found in the fated inevitability of the drama in *Othello* or the unfolding narrative in *Billy Budd.*
Curiously, the epic provokes a less sinister sense of evil than the drama
or the novella, at least to the modern reader. But in all three cases we
find the literary a genuine resource for how we think evil: in all three
works the reality of it looms before us as a ominous, external threat
which, in spite of its potency does not result in the loss of our responsibility.

But it is precisely this externality of evil, clearly distinguished from
our own responsible badness, that is disturbing. Do these reflections
indicate that we can be morally bad, but cannot ourselves be evil? To
suggest this is dangerous. The extent to which evil is a reality that
threatens from without, it must be seen as that against which we
struggle, as an enemy that threatens our existential worth, i.e., our
souls. At the same time we must insist that the threat of evil is that
we become evil ourselves and not merely bad, becoming our own
enemy. This aspect is clearer in *Othello* and *Billy Budd* than in *Paradise Lost*, and moreso in the drama than the novella. It is perhaps
more clearly seen in a Greek tragedy like *Oedipus Tyrannos*, in which
the king's own nobility as a lover of truth turns him into an agent of
his own destruction. It is difficult, however, to see any moral fault
here, the Aristoteleans notwithstanding, since ignorance, at least in
the Christian era, seems to extenuate the king's guilt. Perhaps a bet-

ter example might be Dante's depiction of the lowest level of hell, where an icy lake freezes the souls of those who betray love. Judas Iscariot is there, having become entirely wretched by betraying Christ, hating himself as well as his sin. There are also the haunting novels of self-hatred, such as *The Picture of Dorian Gray* or *Death in Venice*, in which the heros watch themselves become agents of evil.

Artworks are not philosophical essays, however; they are directed toward our passions as much, or perhaps even more, than our reasoning. In all of these literary works the effect on the audience or reader reveals how we feel as well as how we think about evil. In a performed drama the emotional impact is highly pronounced. We note the following sensations: 1) evil threatens, as a sinister force that looms as an enemy to what is noble and good; 2) the origin of such evil can be found both in the character of the villain and the inevitability of the plot; 3) the reality of evil, in spite of its prodigality, does not forfeit or even extenuate responsibility; 4) evil is distinct from mere temptation; 5) the dread that is communicated is passionately felt and not merely rationally identified; 6) this dread need not debase us but can ennoble us; 7) what is dreaded is not the mere loss of life or of what is dear, but becoming evil ourselves—hence we can become both immoral and evil; 8) except in nihilistic novels, the defeat of the hero is rarely complete—he suffers great personal loss, perhaps even life itself, or even yields to the temptation to do immoral acts, but does not lose the existential worth inherent in his struggle and thus retains his capacity to be forgiven, 9) if the work is great, we are touched and moved in singular ways—that is, these are resources of truth that may not be available outside the artwork.

The sense of dread felt by the audience or reader is singularly existential: what threatens is the loss of our own meaning, abetted by our own submission. Even popular entertainments reflect this: the vampire is seen as evil just because his erotic bite changes his victim into another vampire; even to the adolescent the thought of losing one's mortality and hence humanity, in the throes of the compelling passion of lust, seems unsavory. It is not that we will die but that we cannot die that seems so perverse. Science Fiction often depicts the so-called higher forms of life on other planets as intellectually superior, but lacking the warm finitude of our terrestrial humanity, they still remain alien. Perhaps immorality makes us unworthy of ourselves, but evil threatens the very being of ourselves as ourselves. Were this existential mutation to be accompanied by the balm of amnesia its terror would be muted; it is precisely because the victim remembers his original humanity that the anguish is so intense, and the longing to return to the less powerful but more sacred homeland of the species marks the impediments to such return as evil. There is no doubt that in these vernacular entertainments evil is depicted as real, though the metaphysics behind such depiction may be tawdry. There is a not-so-fine line between heuristic metaphor and naive superstition, that should be drawn.

There is a final note to be made about artistic representation of evil. The opening scene of *Hamlet* is set in an atmosphere of mists, mystery and darkness, with eerie portents of ghostly visitation. Horror and magic are evoked historically as parallels are drawn to the death of Caesar, when the dead walked gibbering in the streets; and the birth of Christ, when magic mutes the ills of the preternatural. The reason for this is obvious: to accept the arrival of the ghost the mood must first be set, and typically Shakespeare's genius accomplishes it in a few bold strokes. Evil itself provokes mystery, not so much as the merely unknown, but as the hidden. Evil thrives in the dark, in mists, in subterranean caverns—why else is hell *beneath* the earth and heaven above it? The suggestion here is itself not murky but clear: an essential quality of the ambiance of evil is mystery. It seeks not merely to harm or alter us, but also to confuse, to blind, to addle, to mislead. Not all mystery need be evil—for *Hamlet* appeals mysteriously to the birth of Christ—but the murky darkness of spiritual corruption seems fitting for the unfolding of evil. The first scene of the play might even be called "spooky," which seems almost a child's term. If evil is spooky—or mysterious—what might be called the 'epistemology of evil' now emerges as a necessary approach to the inquiry. For we now must seek a response to the question of our own rationality as it confronts the mystery of evil.

Chapter 8
The Eerie

Sinister, dark graveyards; bare, wintry trees snatching at the unlucky with branched fingers; tombstones creaking with the omen of spectres in the mists; howls, moans, shadows and thunder: these seem the fitting accommodations for evil spirits. Such icons of popular entertainment may seem burlesque, but in their origins they succeed in the creation of atmosphere curiously fitting to our passionate response to evil. Even on the greatest of classic canvases the artist depicts night as the time of evil, winter its season, mist or storm its climate, dark undergrounds its place, and mystery its existential venue. Behind all the fun of Halloween links the uneasy doubt in ghoulish terror. The spooky has its own childish claim on us. These are superstitious manipulations of bawdy sentiment, perhaps; but a Goya painting, Wotan's descent into the Niebelheim in Wagner's opera, a fresco by Michelangelo, belong to the canon of the great; and they too are unashamed in their use of such atmospherics to depict evil.

The iconography of evil is not simplistic, though triteness makes it bawdy. What does it signify that such a venue succeeds? That evil belongs in the realm of spiritual mystery? If we accept this provisionally, what further can we learn? The commonplace adage that we fear the unknown is here irrelevant; the thing that goes bump in the night may be a thief or the wind; our imagination surfs in the foam of ignorance. Even if it be the burglar, it is not mystery or spirit; it is merely a threat, albeit a serious one, that perhaps deserves our fear. Mystery, due to the modern success of a wonderfully companionable art-form, seems to have become a delightful puzzle to be solved, more intellectual than spiritual, made all the more charming by the irresistible character of the sleuth. The delight is in the process of the journey from dark confusion to bring clarity, which is why the best detective thrillers are also comedic. Sherlock Holmes and Nero Wolfe delight by their characters as well as their brilliance in puzzle-solving. A puzzle, however entertaining, is not mystery; an unidentifiable threat, however frightening, is not mystery either. Darkness may be the iconographic milieu of evil, but not because of the ignorance resulting from our not seeing—for once the light is turned on we discover the bump was only the branch blown against the pane—but rather because of what being in darkness means beyond mere opportunistic blindness. In this iconographic sense, darkness is not a metaphor for ignorance, but for mystery.

Not all mystery is malignant. A professor of biology may know perfectly well how babies are conceived, yet still wonder at the mystery of childbirth; post-feminist men may know all the texts of protest, but still wonder at the mystery of a woman; not all the deconstructionist research in the world's academies bar us from awe at the mystery of artistic genius. A mystery, in the spiritual sense, cannot be solved, either by detective or neurologist or art-critic; yet, neither is it a mere emotional feeling, lacking veridical significance. The etymological origin of mystery puts it akin to secrets, i.e., truths kept from the uninitiated and unworthy.

Is there not something of an embarrassment in these reflections? Can we really take seriously an attempt to find philosophical meaning in so juvenile a phenomenon as the *spooky*? Among the pompous there will certainly be no little scorn heaped upon such inquiry. But scorn from the pompous need not deter, and no existential phenomenon is unworthy of inquiry; and if the spooky, the mysterious, and the spiritual seem quaint, the fault lies in the pomposity of the jaded. The legitimacy may shown in the analysis; if it remains juvenile the only loss is the effort expended by the inquirer, but if it yields understanding those who are ashamed to probe into the eerie lose an avenue to truth. With such an option the decision is obvious. There is no shame in asking about this phenomenon.

What attracts us about the spooky? What repels us? Children love to snuggle up with their parents in a darkened room before the fire to hear a ghost story. What happens in such a phenomenon is the contrast. The familiar is enhanced by confronting the alien. The realm of witches and ghosts is not merely scary, as snarling dogs and angry bullies are scary; they are spooky—and this means they represent a way of existing that is not only alien by mysterious. Their secrets are not merely unknown to us; acquaintance with the mysteries bring about a mode of existence that is uncanny, foreign, exiled, lost; in short, homeless. We do not *belong* there; we lose our family, friends, and home. The warmth of the fire, the loving parental arms holding us close, even the sharing of this spookiness with our siblings, these constitute home and hearth, where we belong. But belonging is of supreme preciousness. The spooky is akin to the threat of exile: it puts us where we cannot dwell. Perhaps it is even more dire: it removes all possibility of belonging at all. And this makes home all the more precious.

The existential syllogism now emerges. Childhood stories of ghoulish graveyards and spooky castles inhabited by monsters entertain precisely by contrasting belonging with unbelonging. Evil then becomes a species of homelessness or abandonment. Mystery, in the negative sense is not the merely unknown, but the strange; it is not something to be solved, but dreaded. Mystery in the positive sense provokes awe and a trembling in the face of a secret truth acknowledged but not knowable, or at least not testable; though it must in principle be falsifiable. To say that evil is mysterious is thus to say that it threatens our belonging. But belonging is one of the most important pathoempirical modalities available for philosophical reflection, for it is nothing less than the existential meaning of space.

Space and time are universally recognized as the necessary conditions for finite existence. When sheared of all the baggage of theoretical accounts, space is originally nothing but the ultimate presupposition for making the single question 'where?' possible, just as time makes the question 'when?' possible. These originary questions are without peer, and have no higher ranking presuppositions. When these questions are raised in terms of what it *means* to exist, 'where' provides either belonging or not-belonging, and 'when' provides becoming: either becoming who we are or becoming other than ourselves. "Where," then, is either mine or not mine, ours or not ours. The fundamental, existential phenomenon of belonging is thus made intelligible by the difference between being able to succeed or fail at our own spatiality. Failure at being spatial is the uncanny wretchedness of not belonging anywhere; success is belonging somewhere, even if we are physically absent from that place. Robust adventurers have a strong sense of their belonging; their wandering is not exile. 'Home' is the name given as the basis of our dwelling, and having no home is the eerie uncanniness in which we are in existential exile. The German term 'unheimlich' literally means not at home, and is usually translated 'uncanny' or even 'eerie' or 'spooky'; Heidegger uses this term in connection with his analysis of dread (*Angst*), which he sees as essential for authenticity. It is not Heidegger's employment that matters here, however; it suffices that we realize the seriousness of the phenomenon. It is not a mere abstract possibility that we belong in the world yet also do not belong here; it is concretely real as a modality of our existence.

Neither mystery nor spookiness are of themselves necessarily evil. But it seems curiously apt to place evil in such a milieu, if for no other reason than that such a milieu expands the range of our meaning even as it threatens otherness. Evil is thus once again revealed as a threat to becoming other than ourselves even as it resides within as a part of our conflictive reality. But with the emergence of spiritual evil, the threat is not that we are in the wrong place, but that there is no place for us at all. Evil is spaceless, not in the empty sense of taking place (!) in some extra-spatial realm, but as a threat to our own spatiality: belonging.

The very word 'threat' however also indicates something awry with time, the companion of space as the necessary condition for finite existence. The existential meaning to time is becoming, as Eve becomes Eve through her acceptance of knowing good and evil or Lincoln becomes Lincoln as the burden of his logic compels him to lead the nation from mere unionism to abolition. Who we are is revealed only in our unfolding story; but the story can itself become a non-story, not in death but in distortion of our own becoming, so that we become other than who and what we are—we become alien to ourselves. This loss of identity in our unfolding is not the result of mere immoral acts, but is the self-submission to alien destiny. The spooky lures us to the possibility of becoming haters of ourselves—wretchedness—by letting our story become a non-story, and our space a non-space. Thus, like space, time can become either ours or not ours. In the phenomenon of spookiness the future looms beyond itself becoming a thwart to our own past and present. It is not that we are going to endure a period of hard times, but that time itself no longer unfolds as ours: we have no meaningful time because in evil we have no story. Mystery in its negative sense is timeless as well as spaceless and as such is absolutely alien, even as it lurks within us as a thwart to our becoming and belonging.

It is nevertheless still space, as the existential ground of belonging, and not time, as the existential ground of becoming, that is predominant in the phenomenon of the eerie. It is possible to become radically lost—that is: not lost the way a child is lost is a department store or hikers lost in the mountains, but the way an opportunity is lost forever or, in the religious vocabulary, the way an unrepentant sinner has lost his soul. The power of evil, therefore, threatens to make us lost souls, estranged forever from where we dwell, no longer recognized as a member of our home or people. To lose oneself is to enter the realm of mystery in the negative sense. It is what the child fears when hearing the ghost story: that he will be snatched away from his home. It is an eerie feeling. But "lost" also refers to the vanquished in battle:

> My Portion is Defeat—today—
> A paler luck than Victory—

Later, in the same poem the poet Emily Dickinson adds:

> There's something prouder, over there—
> The Trumpets tell it to the Air
> How different Victory
> To Him who has it—and the One
> Who to have had it, would have been
> Contenteder—to die—   (639, Johnson)

Here, loss means defeat, in which the contender is more contented—magnificent poetic parallel here!—to die. Such language evokes the warrior, where the realm of spirit has long been recognized as both fitting and necessary. Plato, in the *Republic*, argues that the position of the warrior in the state corresponds to the position of spirit in the soul. The sacrifice of the individual's interest for the sake of the community is fundamental for the spirited warrior. The poet spots this by showing the warrior prefers death to loss; not merely because he is ashamed, but because he fails to protect his homeland.

The reference to the warrior's loss shows that the place of our belonging abuts a battlefield, where cowardice is the surest path to being defeated and defeat is the loss of our belonging. The language of spirit becomes the vocabulary of evil. When we speak of evil as a power we do not mean a natural force like gravity, but a spiritual force such as fate or grace. In order to make sense of our existence we must assume the reality of such spirited or even mysterious forces, for how could the story of a life be made intelligible without some sense of fate conjoined with character? How could our stories unfold without the struggles to become who we are against the spiritual forces that would lead us to become other than who we are? The point is not that the Other is always the enemy, but that the enemy is always the Other; and what is lost in the eerie mystery is our dwelling place. The alien now possesses our land. Having lost, we are homeless; and so we tremble.

Confrontation with the eerie often brings about a shivering, as if a chilling draft were fingering our skin, prompting the desire to wrap ourselves more amply with covering garments. The howl in the dark woods raises goosebumps, and we hunch more deeply into our coats. It is not arbitrary that Dante depicts the deepest level of the Inferno, and hence of evil, as a frozen lake, entombing those wretched souls who have betrayed a friend. This phenomenon of shivering at the spooky is revealing in two ways. First, it suggests the icy loneliness of abandonment, far from the warmth and friendliness of the hearth; and Second, it suggests the instinct to cover oneself, not just for warmth but to hide the shameful nakedness of the outcast. Thus, the pitiful shivering of the abandoned is added to the general iconography of the eerie reinforcing the notion that what is at stake is belonging.

Shivering in the wintery gale, and crouching to hide the shame of our nakedness, are both powerful images. None are so cold as those bereft of friends; none so naked as those seeking to hide in shame. The spooky makes us tremble precisely because of these possibilities. Nakedness shared in love is supremely precious, emphasizing the deepest belonging; but as a reflection of shame it shrinks our reality into a trembling knot seeking nothingness. Ostracism into the frigid rejection of the outcast shivers the soul in pitiless abandonment, losing all sense of social warmth. Evil abandons. To be more precise: to become an agent of evil is to endure ultimate ostracism, and hence to become a stranger to ourselves. That we can dread such alienation in no way debases or ignobles us; to confront such possibilities requires courage, and courage is never ignoble.

We do not shiver because we first believe in ghosts; rather, we first shiver, and then allow the stories of ghosts to give a concrete basis for our shivering. Thus, to discredit belief in ghosts, which we must as we grow older, is not to discredit the icy shivering which as a phenomenon reveals what it means to confront evil and the possibility of being its agent. We do not shiver in eerie revulsion at what is bad, but only at what is evil; and the shivering is in part due to the dread that we ourselves may become agents of this reality. The shivering itself is not cowardice; though to take self-pitying protection in the unfairness of having to be bold surely is. Nietzsche is certainly right that to cower before the vague shadows in the mist is unworthy of a free agent; he is wrong, however, in arguing from this truth that evil is therefore an illusion we need not fear. Fear is necessary for courage, and the reality of evil is necessary to keep such fear from being based on an illusion. If the opposite of evil is nobility, as Nietzsche suggests, then both the reality of evil and the reality of fear must be assumed rather than denied for there is no courage—the skeletal basis of nobility—in fearing an illusion or in an illusionary fear. There must be a real dread of a real threat if the confrontation itself is to have any meaning.

The phenomenon of shivering in the face of the eerie or the spooky thus reveals an important insight into the reality of evil and hence the reality of ourselves. This reality does not consist of the occurrence or existence of preternatural entities like ghosts and vampires; rather it pervades our existential world both as a ground of certain truths—such as, for example, that we can be metaphorically marooned on islands cut off from our homeland—and as a non-arbitrary force that influences beyond our creative imaginations. To be the ground of truth and to be independent of our creative imagination is what the word *real* means; it is not necessary to add the requirement that this force or power be the result of a physical entity causing some subsequent occurrence, as the natural power of gravity causes leaves to fall. The shivering itself, as a natural phenomenon, must have natural causes (such as cold weather or psychologically induced reactions), but what is revealed in the meaning of such shivering exceeds the accountability of causal entities. The danger in talking about phenomena such as the eerie is that it will be misconstrued as superstition or magic, that is, a species of "invisible mechanism." Many thinkers seem to believe that when one talks about spiritual reality one is simply talking about causal phenomena that cannot be sensed but is otherwise governed by the same principles that explain sensed phenomena. Magic, after all, is still mechanistic; it's just beyond our ken. Apparently if I were to know what Merlin knows, mixing the right syllables with the right ingredients, I too could change a toad into a prince, just as if Merlin were to have known about electricity he could have built an electric lamp. A primitive who believes that evil spirits have killed his cow would not be surprised to discover the spirit's name was anthrax. Garlic and crucifixes that ward off vampires are understood as mechanistic causes, in principle no different than penicillin warding off bacterial pneumonia or even magnets attracting iron filings. What is called superstition is nothing other than naive causal mechanisms: I may be wrong in believing that if I say the devil's name backward three times I will not be bitten by invisible gremlins; but such belief is still causally mechanistic; there is nothing spiritual about it at all. The fact I do not get bitten when I utter these incantations may even reinforce my false belief, as constant conjunction may often mislead contemporary scientists. It may be the case—as apparently the statistics indicate—that those suffering from threatening ills, who devoutly pray, improve more rapidly and more often than those who do not; but this, too, can be given natural—i.e., psychological—causal accounts, which themselves need not always be accurate. The reality of evil and hence of ourselves as conflictive is thus a spiritual, not a mechanistic one—and hence cannot be either magic or superstition, since these are also mechanistic. Not all accounts of spiritual reality are true; after all, we have contradictory spiritual accounts, so at least some must be false. Critical reflection on the existential meanings of pathoempirical phenomena may well be the most rewarding technique of uncovering these secrets.

I am, however, not two beings, one mechanistic and one spiritual; but one being, whose reality can be disclosed in part by mechanistic principles and in part by spiritual or even existential ways of thinking; and indeed there may be other ways of thinking that reveal who and what I am. Perhaps biotic or immunological accounts require ways of thinking that are not reducible to mechanism, perhaps aesthetic learning reveals beyond these; there is no methodological super-principle that tells us in advance what the explanatory accounts must be. We find that once-accepted ways are sometime discredited by further discovery or reflection, and this, too, is part of learning. The breadth of such possible explanations, however, is no bar to the determination of essentialist analysis, so that it is yet meaningful to understand ourselves as fundamentally in conflict, and that the contenders of this reality-establishing strife are good and evil.

Nietzsche is certainly correct in his realization that once we distinguish bad from evil we must also distinguish two different senses to what the term *good* means. He suggests the opposite of bad is the noble, whereas the opposite of evil is the ignoble or the weak; and there is much illumination in this suggestion. However, with the present discoveries won by the reflection on the ghostly or the spiritual, there appears another candidate. Perhaps the opposite of evil is not (only?) the noble, but (also?) the sacred.

Chapter 9
The Unholy

In a moment of supreme terror, buffeted by titanic assaults on her judgment, careening in a chaos of confusion, Sophie was compelled to make a devastating choice. She must choose which of her two children should live and which die; her failure to choose would result in both her son and daughter being immediately and savagely executed. There was no political or practical reason for this, as if, for example, there were not enough room for all three in the barracks. The imposition of her selection was made solely to place upon her the unendurable burden of knowing she had actually chosen which of her own beloved children would die. They had made her, a loving mother, an infanticide. William Styron's novel, and the film based on it, were aptly titled *Sophie's Choice*. Perhaps it was no choice at all, but a spasm of terror; it does not matter; what matter's is the shredding of all her moral self-respect. It is hideous enough to lose a child under any circumstances; worse to have the child murdered; but entirely eclipsing to be freighted with the yoke of guilt for causing it, even if under duress. Francis Clifford, an underrated writer, wrote a novel, *The Naked Runner*, in which the protagonist Laker, is compelled to murder an innocent man in order to save his son. Can we even begin to understand what it is like to have to decide in such cases? Who would dare censure any judgment made by these hapless people?

Unfortunately, we know—though we would far rather not know—that such appalling cruelty is not only in novels or films. The dreaded secret police of many twentieth-century tyrannies made such terrorist demands frequently on their own citizens. Stalin's NKVD and Hitler's Gestapo knew quite well the best way to enslave a person is to threaten their loved ones. Escaping from or plotting against terrorist governments became almost unendurable with the certain knowledge that one's beloved would be tortured or killed; indeed failing to carry out heinous acts yourself was grimly enforced by the hostage of the precious. Yet, it is not merely the agony and the suffering of the tormented victims that matters here, but the unholy willingness to use such tactics of inhumanity for any sake whatsoever. The Nazi officer who forced Sophie's choice was not even named; he came out of the shrieking darkness as an agency of sheer evil. It is not his personal cruelty that stuns us, but the weltanschauung of the profane. These examples may well be the most evil of all we have considered.

What makes them profane is the turning of our natural instincts toward goodness into an agency of immorality. It is because we love our children that we are forced to unnatural acts; it is because we retain a sense of terrible guilt that we abet the enslavement of ourselves. When the reason one man unwillingly supports the machinery of the hated is mere fear or personal survival, we can understand though perhaps not condone his submission; but when the reason is love itself, and the subsequent anguish a scalding guilt, there is only confusion of the worst kind; for the very patterns of reverence are rearranged into the rack of self-disgust. It seems wicked to be good. Laker's love for his son seems a good thing; to protect him seems the most sacred duty of a father. But this very love entraps him into becoming an ethical monster. When our very goodness becomes bad, when our remaining years stretch out before us as the skin on a drum of shame, beaten hourly in the rhythm of self-hatred, we cannot but loathe our very existence as persons. The dark novels of Graham Greene, John La Carré and Francis Clifford reflected the cold war's perverse reasoning that intelligence agencies even in the democracies could and often did use the very loyalty of their moles profoundly to betray their trust in what they deemed were worthy governments. These literary disclosures of malignant nihilism disturb precisely because the good is transformed into the bad, the virtues become vices, salvation in trust becomes damnation in betrayal. It is not accidental that among the best of these, such as Greene, the moral turmoil is set against the awesome confrontation of the religious. This species of self-revealing is so brutal that language itself cries out for a vocabulary of censure unreached by any except the loftiest; this, we say, is sacrilege.

Can it be that the deeper we plunge into the darkness of evil the clearer it becomes that what is at stake is the sacred? It is not only that the sacred is what is abused by evil, but that evil itself can be real only in the precinct of the holy. The turmoil of the ultimately betrayed, like Sophie and Laker and the all-too-real agents in the feral espionage of belief, seems to shatter the crockery of censure, spilling the soup of moral nutrition, staining the tablecloth of hope. The just and the unjust presuppose redress, but the nihilism of evil assumes nothing save nothingness. When what troubles is the meaningless, only the most meaningful can contain. But why call it the sacred?

We must not be misled here. The sacred is not some mere psychological ranking of our own preferences. Merely to esteem a certain place for its fond memories does not bestow sanctity on it; nor does every account of the universe necessarily include some sense of worship or holiness. A purely natural description of the world is more honest in denying anything sacred than in retranslating it into psychological preferences or mawkish sentimentality. The adolescent delinquent may put himself in harm's way for the piece of turf that his gang claims as their own, but to allow them to say these streets are sacred "to them" is to abuse the term. The youthful gangsters may even have a romantic sense of his own misguided loyalty, and as a trait of his character may even be admired, but the turf is not sacred except in a metaphoric sense, for this would reduce the holy merely to what we hold dear, which is counter to the very meaning of what is truly sacred. In the strictest sense, only the reality of a divine person can bestow the sacred; all other uses are analogic metaphors, though even as analogic they can retain great power. This, I concede, is a severe rendering, emphasizing original etymology in the face of popular usage; but such severity here is needful. The authority of the existential argument should not be unravelled by the softening of so powerful a term. If the claim that the opposite of evil is the sacred is to mean anything, it cannot be watered down to the point where anyone can accept it easily. Perhaps it should not be easily accepted. If it is true, it is a bold claim; it cannot be made more true by making it less bold.

If there be anything at all that is truly sacred, then there must be, however murky our understanding, some supreme personal presence, perhaps necessarily mysterious, that somehow bestows a concrete authority on what it means to struggle with good and evil. The consequent of this hypothetical conditional may be false; but if so, so is the antecedent. What are the bases for arguing in this way? The burdens placed upon both Sophie and Laker reveal that what troubles us about their grisly predicaments is the assault imposed on the personal reality of their moral possibility. They are bewildered precisely because the moral seems hostage to the reality of evil—that is, the towers of morality have been razed into rubble, making the good bad and the bad good. This, however, seems to unbind the ligatures that make us persons. It is not merely that we are morally abused because we are treated like mere things rather than people—which is Kant's profound analysis of immorality—for this happens whenever anyone does something immoral. It is rather that being a person now seems to become something repugnant in itself. We are forced, in the face of this kind of evil, to regret being persons at all. The assault is thus levelled against what it means to be a person. This forces us to reflect on the very bestowal of our personage; we either curse it or entreat it as some final refuge against nihilism. Evil becomes the concrete reality that opposes whatever reality being a person means.

If evil is therefore anti-person, its opposite must somehow be the root or ground of being a person. We cannot explain the origin of persons by anything less than a person, and so the sacred consists precisely in this that a concrete, original, real person is made available. The person as ground of all persons is what theists identify as God; the availability or presence of this supreme person is what we mean by the sacred.

The sacred is therefore the availability of what opposes the anti-person, which is evil. Yet, by the very nature of the ultimate authority of the sacred, it cannot be simply the abstract principles that guide us toward moral behavior. The moral presupposes persons; evil would destroy the possibility of persons; the sacred welcomes the reality of persons. There are two ways that evil assaults the sacred: profanation is the assault form without; sacrilege is the assault from within. The Nazi officer who forces Sophie to choose is profane; the treachery of Judas is a sacrilege. This distinction once more supports the argument that evil is both internal and external. We do not identify the sacred as the divine person, but as that which makes him available to us, not as a factual assertion but as a disclosure of his reality, the way a sacred temple discloses by making available the god within. In this sense, the sacred becomes the ultimate belonging, as both profanation and sacrilege close down the precinct of the holy. Evil becomes manifest as the unholy.

In the presence of the sacred, which itself makes available the presence of the originary person, there is a galaxy of curious responses, including awe, trembling, fear, respect, wonder, perhaps even love. But the most singular is what might be called fundamental gratitude—by which is meant: being grateful for existence itself. We are grateful not only that we exist but that we as unique, irreplaceable persons exist. I can be grateful only to persons; though I can take non-grateful delight in the serendipity of good fortune. This gratitude toward the originary person for my being at all reveals the contingency of my existence: I am, but I need not be; that I am *as* I am is therefore a bestowal that is entirely gracious and for which, in the mode of the awesome, I am thankful. To be thankless is to think on one's own existence as entirely natural, inevitable, and without any existential worth. Oddly, the fundamentally ungrateful often take refuge in the language of rights, as is their own existence were somehow morally imperative. For if they are not bestowed, they must assume some moral need lest they be deemed entirely worthless. This proliferation of rights is based on a naturalist ethics, basing all moral claims on the "right" to satisfy both wants and needs. (If I am hungry I have the right for food.)

The sacred, however, can never be approached through such a naturalist ethics; for if all things of value are mine or should be mine by natural right, there is no need or even legitimacy for being fundamentally grateful. The availability of the divine is most palpably manifest in this phenomenon. It is not fear, as most anthropologists of the primitive assure us is the reason we first kneel down before the sacred, but gratitude. The fear stems from the uneasy realization that, since we deserve neither good fortune nor even life itself, such favor may be withdrawn. Obeisance and reverence is thus given to those points, places, vessels and rituals of contact between the human and divine personage, for in this acknowledgement that we do not deserve, we realize we are favored—a realization both humbling and elevating at once.

If evil be seen as opposed to the sacred, then there can be no evil outside persons or the realm of persons; and persons themselves are more available through the phenomena of grace and gratitude than by wants and needs. The natural is not ample enough to enclose the sacred; and by this declension neither is it ample enough for evil. A world that in principle is entirely explainable by the calculus of nature must therefore be bereft of evil.

To insist that the kindred terms, sacred, profane, sacrilege and holy, presuppose a divine, personal reality rather than mere attitudes of the devout or even a mere supreme being to which the attribute of personage is appended by inference, may seem an arcane and even technically subtle distinction of little interest. But these present reflections constitute an argumentative drift, like some sub-surface current in the ocean persuading ships to veer unnoticed onto an important route of discovery. If the sacred is the opponent of evil, and evil is anti-person and the sacred is the availability of person in the supreme sense, then the current of this drift must be followed. Within the theistic tradition of the west, we find an internecine quarrel that itself contains both the thrust and counterthrust of this oceanic drift. It is precisely because this quarrel is within a theistic tradition that it deserves reflection. It may be helpful to raise the question this way: if the horrors of Sophie and Laker are unholy—and hence profane in the former case and sacrilegious in the latter—how can we best approach what is meant by the holy? We have two models: the theologian and the saint.

The theologian's spinning of conceptual webs to catch the divine fly mocks the love a suffering saint has for the person he knows as God. The saint's sentimental devotion to a supernatural person vexes the respect for reasoning that the mental labors of the theologian have devised. Earnest they both may be—indeed within a single breast they may wrestle—but peace between them comes only, if at all, after the fierce price of a most contentious war. Perhaps the theologian can no more pray than the saint can anatomize his concepts. They are indeed naked wrestlers as in Greek statuary, for they are entirely unarmed, uncovered, shameless and vulnerable; yet they are so intertwined, so palpably close, they may seem, at a distance more like lovers, in an embrace so intimate they are as one. This seeming, however, deceives as well as reveals. The conflict is in true rage.

They both puzzle. To root a love in the brackish soil of self-pitying suffering appears perverse; to act the spider to snare a godly insect shows more elitist arrogance than wisdom. Can a God be webbed in the silks of human conceit? Can a God be neared by the faithless deceit of human affection? And which, webbing or nearing, best describes availability? Is not the theologian silly to think his finite concepts adequate to make available the infinite; is not the religious foolish to feel his own moral passion enough to avail us of the truth? Theology and religion are enemies. And they may both be locked in feral giddiness, struggling over an illusion that has no truth in it beyond their strife. Or perhaps this sacred strife alone is true, at least so far as we, sweating, naked fools in combat, wrestle with truth. If so, the struggle itself reveals the sacred.

The theologians tell us strange things. God is a necessary being whose predicates of perfection are part of his necessity; so he is necessarily good. But a necessary goodness seems anathema to the saint. All the saint knows as good, such as growing, courage, learning, loving, improving, and suffering in sacrifice, do not seem necessary, but bestowed. The theologian's necessary being grows further and further from us, like a departing ship coyly tucking the blanket of the sea over its head until the horizon is straight again. The most real has become the least reachable. If the sacred is the availability of the divine, the language of the theological metaphysician seems singularly unavailing.

If the spider's silk here is language, then what have we done with our words but build a wordy ship to sail beneath a wordy ocean? The word for God, John says, is the Word. A mere word? Do not protest at this, they say; he works in mysterious ways. We are finite, they say, and he infinite, so do not expect to understand. But how, then, do *they* know? Why should we listen to mere words we cannot understand? Yet our poet Auden tells us that 'words have no word for words that are not true.' God is a person, not a shibboleth, in the sense of a spiritual, cultural inheritance, not a concept or principle or force or great first cause, and certainly not just a word. We know what persons are since we are persons too. We can love persons, worship them, talk to them, share with them. If one person happens to be God we are not surprised. In our world persons are far superior in all ways to mere things, for nothing made of mere earth or matter is as real as our own kind, nor can it mean or matter as much. So if God be real or worshipped or loved he must be a person—nothing else qualifies. Not all the spinning galaxies or equally spinning electrons in their trebled billions are as dear or real as one, human sinner.

But here our dreams seem to outrank us. Romance is nice, but sterner truth prevails. Mere emotion cannot make available the truth, so it too seems unsacred. There may be a perfect being, but persons, it seems, are persons just because they can fail, so no person can be "perfect." The nearer the religious brings us to him the frailer he becomes, the more he is felt the less he is thinkable, the more real is the divine, the less divine is the real. The dissembling maxim from all this emerges: if spiritual and moral integrity matter, it is better to "believe" in a personal God; if truth matters, it is more enlightened to postulate a cosmic force, or perhaps not postulate at all. Theism is better for the naive masses; deism or atheism is better for the enlightened elite; theologians are the lobbyists for the latter; saints are the marketers for the former.

There are doubtless devout theologians, but the God to whom Saint Augustine humanly prays and comically pleas in his *Confessions* is not the same God he puritanically describes and seeks to define. So the believer judges Augustine too clever for his own good, the disdainer criticizes him for his anthropomorphic license. This does not eclipse the enmity, but parks it in a single soul, and the rest is torment; possibly unendurable, as it became for the later Augustinian, Luther. The maxim that referees the conflict in this manner has been with us for so long that it fits comfortably, like the old and familiar coat that still keeps the sharp winds at bay. A little superstition, like a fable told before the evening's fire, keeps the family warmly together; the cold critiques of reason are for the unfamilied, enlightened bachelor, preferring severe knowledge to the charms of delusion.

This depiction, though familiar, is mendacious. It is indeed entirely backward, and offends both truth and goodness. For it is not the critical theologian waxing vast, unfelt concepts, or pruning with sceptical shears the leafy extravagances of belief, but rather the culturally luxuriant inheritor of the religiously spiritual who wreaks and not wrecks the truth. There is more truth in our inheritance than in our speculation, even if speculation is part of our inheritance. These last eight words are the deep source of our western, Christian anguish. For the critical no less than the trusting is needful to make available the supreme person and the supreme truth; and hence, though the enmity between the speculative theologians and the devout believer is irreducible, their union is necessary for the availability that is sacred.

The theologian cannot be dismissed as a mere conceptual theorist. An example from history already discussed earlier, may show how fraternal is the strife between worship and criticism. By the third century of our era the church was struggling against a powerful dogma concerning evil, namely the Manichean heresy, which focused on the human body as one of the three sources of evil, along with Satan and darkness, contrasting the three sources of goodness: soul, God, and light. The idea that our bodies are evil is defended by Plato in the

Phaedo and is popular among Hellenistic thinkers, including some Stoics. It also has a natural appeal. It is my bodily urges that lead to improper behavior, from promiscuity and gluttony to idleness and greed. How easy it is to identify the soul as good, struggling against the body as evil. Saint Augustine himself was, prior to his conversion, a Manichean, so the doctrine cannot be dismissed as fanatical or entirely unthinkable. What, then, are the reasons of the early Church Councils that declared Manicheanism to be heretical? Alluring as the doctrine may be, there is one outstanding theological tenet that could not be made compatible with it, namely: the incarnation. If the body were evil, how could God become flesh? The incarnation was the linchpin of Christian thought; it is the supreme doctrine of availability or presence, without it all else was mere Asian mysticism wedded to empty Greek speculation. It was, admittedly, a mystery, but it was fundamental to Christian *thinking*, not mere *belief*. It was also incompatible to Manicheanism, and so the latter had to be vigorously denied as inimical to truth, hence a heresy.

This reflection, however, was not an obscure, picayune, dry, hairsplitting nicety for fusty scholars. It changed radically the very meaning of existence. It was, astonishingly, an anti-puritanical decision that gave the new religion a peculiarly joyous affirmation. We now no longer were required to hate our bodies, or even the urgings, needs, and desires of it. The body, and not just the soul, was able to be good, and as good deserved to participate in eternal reward. But this promise of a corporeal rather than a mere spiritual afterlife was less important than the celebratory, triumphant affirmation of earthly existence, in which love here and now, and not merely hereafter, mattered absolutely. It was this that gave the new religion such a powerful thrust, creating a union or community of the joyous. What deserves amazement, however is its source. The rejection of Manicheanism apparently was the result of a purely theological critique, perhaps the most important in the church's long and contentious history. A theological refinement changed the very character of Christian civilization, including its art, its politics, and daily worship.

The Manichean heresy could not, of course, be blotted out by mere dictate. It emerged again after the Reformation reinstated individual speculation, and in its newer guise, puritanism, it continues to play its role. But that a dry, Fabian, distrustful group of crusty moralists would reject such a powerful and appealing account of evil solely on a fine point of theological reasoning deserves no little admiration. For these historical facts show how theology can and perhaps ought to check and even release the spiritual energies of a great religion. Because of this theological event, ascetism became a minority element in western thought, a dominant one in eastern thinking. The cheerful lustiness of the Wife of Bath now belongs among the robust pilgrims to Canterbury, Falstaff and Sir Toby are dearer than the silly puritans, Malvolio and Angelo and even from the puritanic pen of Milton the carnal joys of the naked Adam with the naked Eve could be gloriously sung. All this apparently follows from the rejection of Manicheanism.

But if the body is not the source of evil then where is it to be located? Here Manicheanism is turned upside down; for it is not the body but the soul—insofar as the soul contains a free will—that accounts for evil. What an inversion there is in this! The body is not bad, but the soul can be. For Calvin, it is even more radical: the human soul must be evil, redeemed *only* by God. Problems of philosophical, and not merely theological consequence, now stun the mind. If soul, and not body is the source of evil, and the soul is created directly by God, whereas the body is procreated by natural laws, then the inference seems to be that a God-created soul alone can be evil. The refinements on this became theodicy, long delayed because of the darkening influence of the vast migrations of savage peoples imploding on Rome. But when it emerged, it met its most artful lobbyist in another puritan celebrating in spite of himself, Milton. Both Augustine, who overcame Manicheanism, and Milton, who transcended his own puritanism, struggled valiantly as warriors against this evil view of evil. And both theologians contribute mightily to the cultural richness, not of a mere theology, but of a religion.

If the sacred is the availability or making present the reality of the divine person, and if evil is its opposite, then evil must be originary with this presence. The reason for this can be seen upon reflection: if we imagine first a flawless world of unflawed men created by a flawless God, we then find ourselves stupidly looking around, trying desperately to find the hole from which evil crawled like an overlooked rat. Such a hole and such a rat could never be found in such a world. Rather, we must understand the essence of evil as anti-sacred—seeking to eclipse the presence of the original person, who is a person only as a participant in the struggle. Whatever else we mean by person, fundamentally we mean a reality not governed solely by automatic or inevitable powers. If persons grant, bestow, yield, forgive, choose, love, and share, they cannot be machines, nor can they be mere powers, nor reductions to, necessary or inevitable force. Inevitability, mechanism, and the automatic are all anti-personal characteristics. Evil, then, emerges as that power within our understanding of reality that is machine-like: inevitable, determined, algorithmic, and grimly necessary. Law-likeness is not in itself evil, but only when it is an impediment to the presence or availability of a person. We cannot deny the inevitable, but we can find its limits. The limit to the inevitable must be the sacred; the forfeiture of these limits is evil.

Limits to the inevitable seem impossible; for what is inevitable cannot be thwarted. To think of all reality as somehow preceding inevitably, either as a fatalism, determinism, or mechanism, precludes the possibility of persons. Yet, our reasoning seems bound to affirm only that which is law-like. Is this not what reason is, the giver of laws? Is not logic nothing else but the recognition of the law-like inevitability of inferences? The extent to which logic, as the form of reason, presupposes implacable inevitability, would seem to suggest that the reality of any person would be illogical. Is this what we are reduced to? Is being logical evil?

Logic admittedly measures only what is inevitable, but of itself does not demand reality be only inevitable, for the logical is not equated with the real. Our senses, for example, inform us of contingent, not necessary, truths. It is not logic that is evil, but the restriction of reality to the inevitability that is measured by logic. There must be inevitability, and to insist there *only* be inevitability would, of course, make persons impossible. The threat of everything being reduced to the inevitable itself is a demand made by the inevitability in reality; it is therefore an original given, opposed by the non-necessary presence of the self-created, anti-inevitable, original person. Accordingly, both the sacred and its opposite, the anti-personal inevitability we know as evil, must be co-fundamental.

Even common understanding seems to support this view. We tend to consider agents of evil as acting solely as machines, without compassion or sympathy. Yet, when isolated in speculative language, the revelation seems shocking. We now have a new insight into the essence of evil: inevitability, or even necessity. It may seem peculiarly odd to metaphysical theologians, for whom the most compelling defense is the ontological argument.

> . . . What praise could they receive,
> What pleasure I, from such obedience paid,
>   When Will and Reason (Reason also in Choice),
>   Useless and vain, of freedom both despoiled,
>   Made passive both, had served Necessity,
>   Not me? . . . . (Paradise Lost, Book III, 107-111)

Milton here seems to defy Descartes' argument in the Fifth Meditation, that the essence of God is his existence, making his fundamental nature necessity. Milton does not deny God may be necessary; he simply denies God is necessity. A God whose essence is necessity could not be a person, and could not then be good. The possibility of God's essence being necessity is precisely that against which the mightiest struggle of all is waged, letting the person be.

It is the presence or availability of this triumphant personage over anti-personal necessity or inevitability that is the sacred. We are grateful not only that this presence bestows on us our own unique personage, but that such triumph be achieved at all. This is the mightiest of all possible achievements, and the most worthy—which is why theists talk about God as both good and powerful in the highest degree.

When we speak of the sacred as the availability or presence of the fundamental person, it becomes obvious that sacrilege and profanation bring about his absence or unavailability. This distancing must be possible in order for God to be a person. Were his absence not possible his presence would be necessary, and if necessary it would be inevitable rather than granted or bestowed. It is precisely because I am grateful for my existence in the worship-modality revealed in the presence that is holy that I must reject inevitability for the sake of grace.

The huge assault against Sophie can only be called profane. It is not merely that the officer treats her as a means and not as an end, but that she herself is forced to turn against her own personage; she collapses under the terrible burden of being a person, and hence becomes unable to dwell in the world. Reality becomes an horrific inevitability; the power of necessity crushes out all possibility of bestowal and gratitude. Her rejection of Christianity is entirely understandable, for she is rendered unable to draw near to what is holy. Yet we, reader or audience, discover in this profanation precisely what evil means: that existential force in reality that is the foe of the sacred, where the origin of person touches the person. The opposite of evil therefore seems to emerge as the sacred, and with this emergence the term 'good' is transformed. Only persons are good; but in the fundamental sense, good becomes the origin of persons. The natural world, conceived mechanistically, has no room for either.

Chapter 10
The Ignoble

The entire architecture of the preceding chapter is swept away by a huge existential cyclone from the Nietzschean North. Or at least, so it seems. The very idea of the sacred irks the Nietzschean as the pitiful whimpering of the ignoble. God must die precisely that man might live; evil is not profane but precious; we must, Nietzsche says, become more and more evil. To entertain the divine is to debase the very meaning of goodness. The origin of evil, apparently, as seen genealogically, lies in the fear of greatness, and consequently is unworthy of the noble soul. One gets the impression that even if God were to exist, Nietzsche would still insist that fearing evil is just a mistake rooted in cowardice. It is simply a repulsive idea. Neither is it real; it is a demeaning illusion.

There is much to attract us in this Nietzschean sweep, and we have noted it in earlier chapters. Our present reflections, however, require a deeper focus, which can be articulated in raising two questions. 1.) If we accept ignobility as the essence of evil and nobility as the essence of good, are we thereby required to deny the *reality* of evil? and 2.) If evil *is* real, can we understand it nevertheless as a kind of baseness? These are not Nietzsche's questions, of course, for he does not consider ignobility to be evil; for him evil is what the ignoble fear as greater than themselves, and hence evil is, as that hated by the base, really nobility itself, which may be why we should become more and more "evil." Since the noble do not hate themselves, they really have no sense of evil at all. We have shown ample reasons to doubt this. The new questions, however, emerge: perhaps, in spite of what Nietzsche says, his insight into the priority of the existential modality of being noble may still provide us with a richer contrast to what evil means, unfreighted by the apparent anthropomorphism in the prior chapter.

It is necessary now to consider at least a sketch of the existentially significant phenomenon of ignobility. There are many characteristics that come to mind, from pettiness, meanness and cowardice to inelegance, vulgarity and insensitivity. Perhaps, however, the most telling, singular quality of the ignoble is their deceit. "We truthful ones,"

Nietzsche's superior blond beasts say of themselves, contrasting the ignoble as anti-truth. Here truth is not merely honesty, but also that sought in philosophic inquiry. The ignoble, by contrast, are not only liars, but fearful of learning; they thrive not only in dishonesty, but willful ignorance. This is to say they seek not only to deceive others (by means of lying) but also, and more ignominiously, to deceive themselves, by shunning the quest for truth. Yet lying, as a species of ignobility, is quite distinct from lying as a moral flaw. The very essence of what it means to lie seems to be different when viewed from the moral rather than the existential viewpoint. If lying is a fundamental characteristic of ignobility, it needs to be examined critically.

In *Heart of Darkness*, Marlow explains:
". . . You know I hate, detest, and can't bear a lie, not because I am straighter than the rest of us, but simply because it appalls me. There is a taint of death, a flavour of mortality in lies—which is exactly what I hate and detest in the world—what I want to forget. It makes me miserable and sick, like biting something rotten would do."
These last five words are stunning in their revelation. The simile provokes a most profound revulsion: to bite into something rotten inspires an instinct not only to spit the offending taste from our mouths, but to realize the appetite for food has turned against us, not as a sustainer of life but as a step toward death. Yet, the simile in not merely a tocsin against the toxic, but a profound rejection of what is distasteful. The rotten is spit out not only because it might make us ill, but because it offends taste. We should, I think, take Marlow at his word and accept that this hatred of lying does not depend on his being "straighter" than his audience. He claims no moral superiority in his detestation of dissembling; it is rather judged as something rotten. It is ignoble. In the novella this quotation takes on singular significance since later Marlow lies to the young woman enamored of Kurtz. If he is so offended by lying, why does he not tell her the truth? He has not changed his mind; even at the end lying is still like biting into something rotten; the need to lie to her provokes no little self-loathing. The truth about Kurtz, though, is apparently rooted in far too great a horror.

Contrast this revulsion against lying, which is admitted as being a non-moral rejection, with Kant's analysis, for whom lying is always prohibited precisely because, second only to promise-breaking, it is paradigmatic of immorality. To lie treats others as means and not as ends; when universalized it contradicts itself. It is therefore simply wrong—immoral—to lie. Both Marlow and Nietzsche's blond beasts refuse to lie because it is ignoble; the Kantian refuses to lie because it is immoral. One might object that since both views condemn lying why should it matter? We know lying offends and that we shouldn't do it, so the origin or the venue of its censure is irrelevant. But the venue does matter to the philosopher.

Conrad's Marlow deserves closer analysis. Though lying is repugnant to him, he is compelled to mendacity precisely because defiling Kurtz's beloved with the horrors of the Congo are even more repugnant. It is not the *act* of lying, but the ignobility of being a deceiver that is measured by his existential revulsion; but there is also the ignobility in spreading horror to an unprepared and vulnerable gentility. We do not judge this revulsion in terms of his adherence to certain moral principles, articulated as propositions which are true or false. He is true to his character: he is appalled by the ignobility of the "rotten" as well as the "horrible." His sensitivity evokes in the reader a certain sympathy or even admiration for this deeply troubled man; without the anguish the story would not succeed.

Mendacity in the guise of hypocrisy troubles another literary character. Arthur Dimsdale prefers truth to deception as does Marlow. He aches to be up on the scaffold with Hester, where the public confession of his adultery would ease his soul. Yet, Arthus bears the dreadful opprobrium of his deceit for an outstanding reason: scandal. He is tormented not only by his guilt for being an adulterer, but also for his own necessitated hypocrisy, deceiving his flock lest his flock deceive themselves. Scandal vexes the conscience and thwarts all trust in spiritual leadership. It is only after this same, fickle public learns of Arthur's suffering that they can, and apparently do, forgive him for his sins. As in the case of Marlow, the decision to lie in no way eases the repugnance to lying; but as noble men they accept that burden to avoid an even more burdensome repugnance: the spreading of evil.

An objection that can be brought against both Marlow and Dimsdale is that their reluctant lying is condescending, treating the deceived as too fragile to bear the harsh burden of truth, thereby reinforcing their status as inferiors. This objection may have some validity, but not enough to dismiss the anguish of the two heros; indeed the objection, though perhaps supported by the pure Kantian

critique, founders on the very rocks that support the existential dis-
taste for dissembling. We know that under the banner of anti-hypoc-
risy, honesty is often transmogrified into ignobility. We bare our
souls—and even our bodies—in unseemly displays, airing to a jaded
public all our pecadilos and even felonies, as sops to salacious curios-
ity and the titillation of gossip. This grossness diminishes esteem and
respect; when even the noble are exposed as rutting in the same trough,
the ideal becomes dishonesty, the refined are simply veneers of deceit, we all are *really* vile, and any attempt to pretend there are higher
levels is dismissed as hypocrisy. Under the influence of this wanton
commonality, all refinement and nobility is lost.

   This is the true effect of scandal. Scandal exists, and even in an age
of instant barbarism, like instant cocoa—just add water to the powder, and stir—the pain and loss are serious. But if the price of avoiding scandal is deceit, as it usually is, are we not in a truly vicious
tension? Perhaps the rabble are right: all privacy and decency are at
bottom nothing but cowardly prevarications, covering the truth of
our own gross natures. The fig-leaf is the origin of civilization, but in
covering our nakedness it makes us ashamed. But shame itself is
shameful; we should throw the fig-leaf away, for we are all naked
under our guises, and disguise dissembles. If, in order to keep the
illusion of decency alive I must deceive, then it seems baseness triumphs. The drooling avidity of the scandal-monger is surely not
prompted by any respect for truth; we need not be so blind as to be
taken in by such mockery—using truth itself as a foil for the contempt for truth. Yet, the painful paradox still rankles. Is not deceit,
no matter how judiciously employed, ever a thwart to nobility?

   There are some who grasp the opposite horn of this dilemma. A
kindred spirit, Oscar Wilde, in his *The Decay of Lying*, argues that a
certain anti-puritan spirit of levity is fundamental for the establishment of a noble society. Touchstone tells Audrey that "the truest poetry is the most feigning", a line that Auden uses as title to one of his
more endearing poems. Winston Churchill argues that the truth is
so precious it must be protected by a conspiracy of lies. Perhaps our
original detestation of lying is itself a lie. We should not trivialize
this. Not even Kant in his fiercest rage would censure the "lying" of
poetic hyperbole, for that is but a literary figure. Wilde's protest is
deeper. To be able to lie seems to be the very basis of language—
insofar as language is not mere communication—and hence of cul-

ture. It takes no art, nor skill, nor cunning, nor genius to tell the truth. Perhaps to revere truth itself is possible only in advanced cultures in which lying, like high tariff walls, protects. The above analogy with the fig-leaf may reveal more than it seems, for nakedness, like truth, is possible only when the shame of concealment unconceals. "Who told you were naked?" God asks Adam. The paradox is blinding in its brightness: the natural Adam was never naked, though he wore nothing. Being naked is an existential awareness, in which the need to conceal reveals—as it makes possible—our shame. But unshamed, we cannot be naked at all, and hence cannot be revealed at all.

Curiously there is a greater kinship between the puritanical truth-teller and the ignoble liar; there is greater proximity between the merry mendacity of the poet and the noble truth-teller. The latter pair affirm their existential worth, the former tremble before their own moral weakness. How are we to extricate ourselves from this seeming paradox? It is precisely because the puritanical truth-teller as well as the ignoble liar think in terms of prohibition, rules, and moral measuring, that they seem spiritually akin. How are we to understand the kinship of the noble truth-teller and the custodians of gracious lying? These reflections on the paradox of lying and the revealing nakedness of shame suggest an opening. It is possible to cut through the tangle of these opposing sentiments and suggest an existential essence, to wit: ignobility is a gratuitous enmity against the worth of being a person. The key term here is 'gratuitous'. The noble are gracious in their superiority; they bestow without commerce, giving what is unearned on the basis of abundance. The ignoble, therefore, are rooted in the negative side of bestowal, as when we speak of a gratuitous insult or spiteful pettiness. There is no practical justification for such hurts; they simply spring from the low and bitter sullenness or an envy-inspired hatred belonging to the pitiful.

The origin of gratuitous enmity is therefore conceived as a species of deprivation. The ignoble are envious because they lack; they are mean because, rather than seeking to achieve something better for themselves, they seek to deprive others of their superiority. They endeavor to establish a commonality not by raising the lowly but by lowering the lofty. Being low, their weapons are those of the sniper or guerilla; their character is jealous, revengeful, and egalitarian. Thus described, they seem unworthy foes, like yapping curs, whose dole-

ful whining can be silenced by a good, swift kick. Except for one
thing.

Their guerrilla enmity is focused on the worth of being a person;
and since being worthy is fundamental to all moral judgment, the
enmity of these lowly curs cannot merely be batted away like annoy-
ing gnats. The threat is simply too dire. The attacks from the ignoble, like some mutated virus, outmaneuver the immunological
defenses, and by sheer evolutionary ubiquity, bring down the healthy
host. What is at stake in this struggle of the noble against the ignoble
is similar. Though distinct from the case of the sacred versus the profane, the former challenges the possibility of being a person, the latter the worth of being a person. The enemy of the sacred is shown to
be inevitability; that of the noble is deficiency, manifested in envy-
sponsored egalitarianism. The deficiency of the ignoble is not that of
mere benefits, for the noble are noble in part precisely by their ability
to rejoice in another's success without envy; what is lacking in the
ignoble is the graciousness to let others or even themselves succeed,
or even to let any person *be*, as worthy.

The deficiency of the ignoble is not quantitative but qualitative:
there is an existential *mode* of lacking that contrasts to the existential
mode of possession. The noble can, in the physical sense, be entirely
impoverished, the ignoble can teem with mighty wealth, yet the latter still is in the mode of deficiency, the former of abundance. This is
not a mere emphasis on the virtue of generosity, for being generous is
by no means the same as being gracious. One might, out of a sense of
pity, be generous to the poor, who would gladly receive his alms but
recoil at his pity. One can also be generous ignobly, as when unearned gifts render the weak dependent, or when the giving is rooted
in the desire to be liked. There is dark suspicion of those who purchase companionship, a form of largesse that usually provokes contempt from the recipient rather than gratitude, as every whore-mon-
ger knows well. These examples, however, may distract; the gracious
is different even than the truly generous, for generosity is a virtue
that, when acquired, makes us ethically, and perhaps even morally,
better; graciousness makes us existentially worthier. By declension,
ungraciousness makes us existentially unworthy.

It is gracious to forgive, precisely because mercy stems from a reverence for who one is rather than what one does; the ungracious
cannot forgive precisely because he is unable to go beyond the act.

This inability to go beyond the act is the basis for revenge, as Nietzsche points out. Though his characterization of revenge as the unhealthy hegemony of the past—a point hugely celebrated by Heidegger's analysis—is misleading. It is not the past as an existasis of *time* that ignobles us by its hegemony, but rather the hegemony of the act as act, barring any access to the person who is guilty of the act, and who in his guilt is thus more significant, and who can, as person, be forgiven.

Because ignobility is gratuitous in its attack on the worth of our being persons it cannot be accounted for merely as a violation of moral precepts, and hence becomes a candidate for being the core of evil rather than immorality. Since it has been shown to consist of an existential lack, its candidature resonates with profoundly traditional accounts of evil. Augustine defines evil as non-being or metaphysical deficiency, and in a more cautious way, so does Aquinas. It may seem curious that Nietzsche should share a negativist view of evil with Augustine and Aquinas; but there is a strong persuasion in such thinking. For these christians, if a good God is supremely real, then his opposition would be unreality; for Nietzsche, if the origin of the good as noble lies in the affirmation of one's worth, evil would be the cowardly negation of it. In either case, evil is not real, it is a threat to or thwarting of the real. Nietzsche's own view seems even more radical in the denial of real evil: it is not merely that evil is *opposed* to reality, but it is itself a gross distortion of what it means to have worth. *Only* the ignoble believe in the reality of evil in their craven hatred for superiority.

Centering evil in ignobility therefore seems to forfeit the possibility that it is real. The answer to the first question raised at the onset of this chapter seems to be in the affirmative: yes; if the ignoble is the essence of evil then we must deny evil is real. The second question now must be raised: if evil is real, can we nevertheless see it as a kind of baseness? The difference between these two questions is subtle but profound, for it is possible that evil could be a species of baseness without the metaphysical apparatus. In other words, it might be possible to argue in the following way: evil is real, but its manifestation is to be found in ignoble or base behavior, which is still distinct form immoral behavior. What attracts about this suggestion is the phenomenological wealth learned from the analyses of the sort carried out thus far in the chapter. The base liar seems different from and more repugnant than the robust and merry mendacity defended by

Oscar Wilde and found in the likes of Falstaff or Sir Toby Belch. Precisely because we can distinguish between the noble and ignoble liar shows there is a difference between immorality and ignobility, and there seems good reason to categorize the latter as evil and the former as bad. The question of the metaphysical status of evil can be left to the speculators.

Perhaps. It is not that easy to shelve metaphysics, ever. But even if we could, the suggestion that evil lies at the basis of ignoble behavior is troubling. What then lies at the basis of *immoral* behavior? Badness? But then both bad and evil are equally real. Are there four realities: the bases of bad behavior, good behavior, noble behavior and ignoble behavior? This inflation of realities tends to obscure the whole point of the original distinctions, as well as to regress to discredited, ontical metaphysics. The Augustinian notion of evil as negation or negativity begins to seem more attractive. However, to escape the ignominy of multiplying realities merely to serve a suspect metaphysics, the negativity that may lie at the basis of ignobility would have to be seen existentially.

Heidegger, for example in *Being and Time*, argues that authenticity itself is grounded in guilt, which is defined as "being the basis of a nullity or not-ness." Without the burden of being able to be guilty, it is impossible to manifest the meaning of existence, which possibility is authenticity. Guilt, which is morally negative, becomes existentially positive, since it places the ability to fail within ourselves, thus making us responsible and hence free. Yet, it retains a negative sense even existentially, for it is the basis of nullity or not-ness. Being able to be guilty is thus the supreme possibility of escaping what Heidegger calls the "they-self" in which we lose our own meaning in the noisy clatter of distraction. Perhaps then it is possible to identify ignobility and hence evil as a form of negativity which nevertheless has existential reality.

This suggestion however is laced with peril. There can be no doubt that there are ignoble people who deserve to be censured and who may also be evil in some way. But the extensive reflections on the enormity of evil do not seem sufficiently illuminated merely by ignobility. The discoveries in this chapter have indeed shown that there is an autonomous censure, beyond mere moral indictment, levied against ignobility; but it does not follow that such ignobility is either real or evil. Both immorality and ignobility are based upon the prior reality of a person, and hence are judgments about already real persons; but evil is a co-fundamental reality necessary to make a person possible even as it strives to make persons impossible. This is what is meant by the suggestion that evil threatens the possibility of being a person whereas ignobility threatens the worth of being a person. The possibility of something grounds its reality; the worth of something presupposes its reality.

The prior chapter on the unholy, thus, for all its anthropomorphic dangers, supports the claim that evil is real far more effectively than the present chapter which seeks, vainly, I think, to establish ignobility as the reality which is evil. Perhaps ignobility could be the ground of evil, but then evil is not real; it is a mere judgment based on the reality of persons. The violations of the sacred, profanation and sacrilege, reveal an evil that is real. There are converse arguments as well. Being good rather than doing good (morality) may well include being noble, but the reality of it is the holiness that reveals the sacred. We have, however, not entertained the candidacy of ignobility as the possible essence of evil merely for the sake of dismissing it. It is no small matter to discover that the ignoble threatens the worth of being a person, for such discovery reinforces the fundamental priority of what it means to be a person. There may be many assaults against us as persons, but not all seek to undermine the very worth of being a person as ignobility does, nor the very possibility of being a person as evil does.

It may be helpful to suggest a kind of taxonomy of these assaults. Immorality violates the rules that govern the conduct of persons; wickedness is a quality of one's character that erodes the appreciation of the dignity of persons, ourselves and others. Thus we say *we* are wicked and we *perform* immorally. Ignobility assaults the worth of being a person, which allows us to debase ourselves and others, so that we judge persons as not mattering. But we are *agents* of evil when we assault or undermine the very possibility of being persons. These distinctions are fundamental and should be kept keenly honed in our philosophical inquiry. But their distinctiveness does not imply radical independence. Those who perform immoral acts may well, by the habituation of them, result in our achieved indifference, which may—though not necessarily—change our character to the point of wickedness. Ignobility may so debase our conscience that we find no brake upon our instincts, which turns us into haters of our own moral significance. With such hatred or contempt, conjoined with the wickedness of character, we may find ourselves agents of evil. But only this last can be said to be real, for it is a counter-force to our ability to be persons at all. In the previous chapter this reality was exposed as inevitability, which necessarily resides as essential for our very being. We are, to some extent, mechanisms, and machinery functions inevitably or necessarily; but we are capable of resisting total reduction to this inevitability; and this resistance is a struggle which establishes the reality of our being a person. Immorality, wickedness, and ignobility are all possible because of their primordial reality, but unlike evil, they assume the prior reality of persons. Evil is a force that undermines our possibility of being a person, but we ourselves can become agents of evil by ceding this possibility to its counter-enmity. It therefore becomes impossible to account for evil solely in terms of some personal flaw, weakness, or disposition. It is always, at once, both internal and external; but for the sake of the present discussion it is the *externality* of it that matters. Wickedness, ignobility and immorality are entirely internal. It is precisely because of the externalist dynamics of evil that we can never go beyond it. We are always this side of evil.

It is always risky at this, the highest level of thought, to make analogies, since there can be no true analog to reality. With this caveat, however, it is possible to make an entirely heuristic analogy in order to show how taxonomic ranking can map on to ontological discourse. Among crimes against a legal order we can distinguish between misdemeanors and felonies, just as in ecclesiastical matters theologians distinguish between venial and mortal sins. But in the legal realm there emerges among the felonies a special kind of crime, treason, which must be sanctioned with extraordinary harshness, not because its victims are more seriously injured, but because the crime itself undermines the very institution of punishing crimes at all. Were there no state, there could be no crime whatsoever, since crimes presuppose states. Treason is thus, formally, a singularly virulent felony, since, if unchecked, it renders all other crimes unsanctioned. History shows us that governments lax about treason invite self-destruction, as the Karensky government so fatally discovered in its laxity against the Bolsheviks. The point to be made here is formal: the *real country* is not threatened by interviolations of its government's laws, since crime and punishment are ways of belonging to the formal state and dwelling in the real country; but treasonous revolution is not within the state, but is grounded in a reality outside the country. It is for this reason that we *revere* the Constitution more than the laws passed by the various legislatures, but *love* the country in which we dwell. Treason is against the reality of our communal existence; and though there are laws against treason we think of traitors the same way we think of foreign invaders: as external threats against which an army must be mobilized rather than a mere crime against which the police can be brought to bear. An agent of evil is analogous to the traitor, the immoral is analogous to the criminal. The traitor is within our midst, and hence is an internal threat, but is also the agent of an alien enemy, which is thus also an externalist threat. The nation itself, manifested in its constitution, is real, and as real is the ground of individual laws that serve to protect the citizens and values of a people. The alien enemy is also real, and the agent of that reality, especially in the figure of the traitor-spy, is analogous to the agents of evil.

Further than this the analogy is pressed only at the risk of further confusion rather than clarity. The issue deserves a brief, but independent, reflection.

Chapter 11
The Reality of Evil

We are witness to the unspeakable.

It is the sheer enormity of its assault and outrage on our reality that demands evil, too, be real. There can be no illusion here, no local set of statutes, no quaint traditions and customs, no mere violations of values. It is not enough to say of these outrages that they merely ought not to have happened. The assault upon our witness and our judgment in the face of evil is autonomous; it is other than us; its threat is dire; our trembling before it is not an indictment of cowardice; it were indeed foolish not to tremble. That we ourselves can be transmogrified from its confrontation into its agency is an horrific possibility. Far more than stars and rocks, atoms and cells, daylight and darkness, evil is real. Whatever destroys us, denudes us of worth, overcomes our very possibility, must be real. If not real, what would it be? An illusion? A belief? A value? Values and beliefs are subjective; they are contrasted by worth and knowledge, which are objective; they can change, vary from time to time, and alter from place to place. But the dread presence of the completely inimical cannot be avoided or repackaged into perspectives or any other subjectivist appraisal. Those who assure us there is nothing to fear absolutely are as fanged adders, lulling us into the comfortable delusion that all is well because nothing matters as much as that. There, of course, is the crux. We do matter, perhaps absolutely; or at least our struggles do; and if we matter, if we are real, then whatever would render us unreal must be as real as we are. We cannot all be undone by mere illusions, unless it be the illusion there is no evil, that *it* is unreal.

Whatever human folly is, it cannot be surpassed in its silliness than the orgulous impudence in denying the reality of evil. Yet, in the spirit of our age, we find all the putative sages persuading us that reality is entirely bereft of evil. How can tiny bits of mindless matter, flitting around a most disciplined space, have anything threatening in it, once it is known? They are right in that. If the real is naught but particulate matter, evil has no status. And if this be so, the outrage at the infanticides and the cruelties and the treacheries is itself but a passing spasm on the network of our nerves. It is this folly that the mightily abused, the trembling truth-seeker, the victim and the witness, all refute. We may as well deny the drowning ship the reality of the ocean.

How are we to understand this folly? What is it, in other words, that leads us to deny the reality of evil? The victims of the Nazi holocaust are appalled at the subsequent generation's insouciance. Yet that victim-generation itself, prior to the horror, was in part victimized so easily because of its own insouciance. It seems an almost natural disposition of the human race to trivialize the possibility of evil when time or circumstance affords us any distance from it. There may indeed even be something healthy about this, for brooding over past wrongs or future disaster may itself distract from the possibility of present joy. Parts of the world, such as the Balkans, seem inordinately cursed with such long memories that centuries-old depredations still rankle, causing new hatreds or even wars. Were it not better to forget the outrages of the sixteenth century to achieve at least a semblance of peace in the twenty-first? Yet, though there be prudence in such advice, we cannot prefer forgetting to remembering; history does teach.

It seems, however, a special kind of forgetting that forgets evil. This is not due to an ignorance of facts, or even a dulling of imagination. It is part of evil to conceal itself, to explain itself away. With stunning avidity we seize upon pseudo-explanations of evil so lame that were any other issue at stake the effort would be deemed pathetic. We do not seem so avid to deny the legitimacy of moral censure or the wickedness of character. Most of us seem to accept the notion of responsibility, even if during games of speculation we may pretend to deny it. But though we accept immorality and wickedness, we seem to shun the reality of evil. This tendency is due in part to the realization that if evil is distinct from immorality and wickedness then it must be real, and it is the reality of it we mistrust. This reluctance to accept evil is also rooted in its darkness, or its distance. The holocaust was long ago; it was perpetrated by people entirely other than ourselves, possibly by men entirely mad. So too, with the Soviet gulags, though they were more recent. The genocides in Cambodia were even more recent, but that occurred "over there", again, possibly by madmen. Ethnic cleansing in Bosnia, even closer and newer, simply does not belong to our safe world. How close need it be? How recent? The bombing in Oklahoma City? We still hesitate.

The victims grow frustrated with our naivité. We grow more enamored with speculative theories that explain away evil, regardless of
how foolish and inane they be. Are we just stupid?

Perhaps we are not stupid but stupefied. The naive are entirely
unprepared for the sneakiness and power of evil, and when it van-
quishes, we are left as hurt and abused children, stunned into a cruel
dislocation. Nothing separates more than the victim of evil trying to
awaken in the unalert a realization of its reality. Perhaps like sex and
the taste of raw oysters it must be directly experienced to understand
it at all. We are comfortable with our wrongs, our crimes, our sins;
but to speak of evil as a reality, and our possibly becoming agents of
this reality, upsets a certain manageability, which, in its beguiling
familiarity, blinkers our metaphysical vision. This dissembling naivité
is a web of deceit woven by the power of evil itself. It could not even
be evil if it did not stupefy, and if fatal naivité is necessary for such
stupefication, then the self-deceit inherent in denying the reality of
evil belongs to its nature.

There are genuine, dire threats to which few attend with alarm.
Churchill's lonely voice against the rise of Hitler was disregarded, to
our chagrin. Orwellian protests against the tyranny of Soviet cruelty
were disdained to our regret. Thoughtful Romans of the fourth century sounded the tocsin against the impending collapse, and few lis-
tened. Two strategies of deafness always rise up during the fleeting
periods of opportunity to avoid disaster: the first is the prolixity of
false alarms, like the boy in the fable crying wolf. The second is the
amused but false appeal to the putative eternality of parental genera-
tions lamenting the impiety of the young. Modern non-alarmists cite
Aristophanes to show that every generation fears the rebellion of its
children. But Aristophanes' generation had every right to feel alarm,
for the corruption was real, and soon led to the collapse of the em-
pire. In the sixties and early seventies America placed its hopes on the
young, all trust and natural goodness was located in the long-haired,
gentle rebels, not in the experienced adults who were seen as tired
reactionaries; and the consequences ranged from disappointing to
dreadful.

It is undeniably bad strategy to over-vilify. The film *Reefer Madness*
endorses the use of marijuana by the silliness of its censure against it.
Medical horror-stories about the putative ills of masturbation serve
to mock the moralizing of all medical science. Fascination with the

grim corruption of our polity blared and beaming at us from the boxed tubes, jades even the adolescents, who learn an assumed melancholy as reason for despair, indifference, and narcotic escape. In these cases, the reality of evil, the seriousness of dire threats, as well as the life-affirming virtues that counter them, are all muted by the tactics of disingenuity. To confront the possibility of radical failure seems comically alarmist; to trust in classic virtues like honor, nobility and loyalty, seems outdated and uncool.

Against such intransigence, those who have confronted the reality of evil endure a frustration almost as overwhelming as the evil itself. It is bad enough to have suffered under the lash of cruelty, but it is insulting to be placated by soft assurances of its unreality. There is more here than the mere virus of relativism, insidious though that may be. It is more akin to nihilism; but even this refining of labels misses the point. Must only the burned know of the fire? Even those who acknowledge the reality of evil are not thereby free of its power. Nietzsche is certainly right in his censure of the melancholic naysayer and despiser of the human race. The morbid are no more enlightened than the naive optimist; they both offend by their almost criminal blindness to what it means for there to be evil. Its reality cannot entail its inevitable victory; if evil is real so is its opposite; the reality of goodness is denied only by the foolish; that goodness can triumph over evil is so magnificent and palpable a truth that only the basely blinkered can gainsay it.

These observations about the ease with which the reality of evil is dismissed are important, since such dismissals constitute part of the general strategy of evil, and thereby reveal counter-strategies by the commanders of goodness in the great strife that discovers what it means to be a person.

The alarmists, who seek to waken a realization of evil's reality may, for all their sincerity, fall to the gambit of their foe; for in girding against the dreadful we become dreadful ourselves. To don the armor of puritanic intransigence commits the grave martial folly of so many defeated generals: the theft from offense to enrich the defense; to rely on Maginot lines in an era of tanks and planes; to build barriers against the evil enemy rather than attack-regiments to defeat him. For what is the nature of this warfare? In the analysis of the unholy it is noted that the essence of evil is the assault on the possibility of being a person; this anti-person force is recognized as inevitability, that of the pro-person force consists in all those attributes that transcend the inevitable: forgiveness, generosity, bestowal, grace, beauty, love, nobility, and laughter. The grim cannot be defeated by greater grimness, nor the inevitable by newer algorithms of inevitability. To be on "this side" of evil rather than on "that side" or "beyond" it is to unsheathe our own swords and slice into the fray boldly, to forge weapons from the arsenal of our own reality that allow us to seek out the enemy and defeat it, through never to destroy it completely. To seek the truth about evil requires some sense of what it means to be good. If the metaphor here is martial, this means: not all our weapons are defensive—perhaps not even our best weapons are.

The suggestion that perhaps the very metaphor of war is incompatible with the gentler anti-inevitablist attributes of being a person, must be rejected. It is far more powerful to forgive than to offend, to bestow with graciousness than to yield to imperatives, to be gracious than demanding, to love than to hate, to laugh than to denounce, to celebrate beauty rather than to fear its distraction. It is not merely nicer and more pleasant, it is more powerful; it demands greater strength and reveals greater truths. If there be an all-powerful, its strength could not be caught in the nets of utility. This realization of the power of being a person reveals the weakness in the anti-theodicist argument, even as it undermines the folly of the theodicist himself. The martial metaphor is indeed apt once we realize the positive (pro-offense) power of the good in the struggle with evil.

There is doubtless a paradox here. On the one hand we note the ease with which the reality of evil is denied; on the other we note that the struggle against evil requires the husbanding of non-alarmist qualities that seems deaf to these very alarms. Is not love a curious warrior? It seems even odder to clepe these personalist weapons as offensive rather than defensive. Or perhaps the point is irony rather than paradox. Artful irony alone can reveal some of the deeper mysteries of what it means to be a person; the love-soldier often is more savage than the sentinel of duty. It may be irony that teaches us that comedy, not tragedy, best exposes our weakness, that forgettors of evil forget the good, that alarmists waken the enemy as well as the town, that those weary of the struggle lengthen its tenure, that the gentle is not soft but hard, that the fearless lack courage, and only the fearful dare to be brave. If these are truths that irony reveals, then the reality that makes them true must seem to the non-ironic ironically unreal.

The philosopher, however, must seek to understand what reality means. As a lover of truth he is quite willing to recognize irony as one of its sources, but as rational critic he must probe even as he trusts. To say evil is real is not to say it is a physical entity or force, such as gravity; nor need he anthropomorphize evil into a personal Satan. Perhaps it need not even be an entity at all, as both Kant and Heidegger have shown in their critiques of either "speculative metaphysics" (Kant) or "ontic thinking" (Heidegger). To be real is to satisfy two conditions: it must be independent, in some way, of our creative imagination; and it must be the ground of truth. In distinguishing evil from other terms of censure we note that our own personal reality is the ground of those truths that make up moral censure as well as the censure of wickedness in character. Thus the immoral and the wicked are grounded in the reality of persons, which grounding accounts for whatever truth there is in such judgments. But the reality of persons themselves is understood in terms of the reality of good in conflict with the reality of evil. Evil thus serves as an indirect ground of the immoral and the wicked, but as a direct ground of the reality of persons, which is understandable fundamentally as the strife between the gracious (good in its fundamental, transmoral sense) and inevitability (evil). The realities of both fundamental good and fundamental evil must themselves be understood existentially; and they have already been revealed in part by the reflections on such modalities as ignobility, sacrilege, and outrage.

The assaults against us are not trivial; the possibility of radical defeat is both palpable and genuine. The opiate of the people is not religion but the narcotic blindness to the reality of evil—though to be sure, inauthentic religion is a part of that blindness. Those aware of evil are desperately conscious of the almost implacable lethargy that blinds, deafens, and anaesthetizes us against accepting it as real. Yet in spite of this—perhaps: ironically?—the conflict continues, and even among ordinary people the warrior virtues and the joyous affirmations of what it means to be a person emerge as triumphs. Beleaguered by a cosmic grimness and a long history of silly despair, we nevertheless find the resources to celebrate our folly in warm comedy, thrill to the learning that endears us to truth, forgive unanswered wrongs and thereby vanquish revenge, and love even in the face of insolence. The battle is already underway before we are born.

The strategies of the ordinary are thus truth-revealing and hence evil-defeating; but the philosophical passions are still distinct. The antics of the metaphysician may amuse the on-looker, as servant-girls laugh at Thales, but theirs is a profound folly, not unlike the love-addled suitor who woos comically but with an ardor that may win his suit. As thinkers, the nature of reality matters, and if evil be fundamental, the quest for comprehension will, like Orlando, persist in spite of Jacque's scorn. We have marked some attempts: the body may be the reality that is itself evil, though this Manicheanism is rejected by both theologians and Nietzschean neo-theologians as heresy. Human nature itself is evil say the early theological reformists, especially Zwingli and Calvin. But their own contemporary followers do not follow them in this. The most persistent realists, however, are the metaphysical voluntarists, who find in the freedom of the will the fundamental reality that accounts for evil. All these thinkers reveal a profound instinct to isolate a reality that is itself evil, for unless reality is somehow the basis or foundation of evil, the struggle is mere illusion. A more critical look at the voluntarist metaphysician reveals the complexity inherent in any attempt to a reductionist account. If this noble enterprise fails—if, that is, the voluntarist metaphysician is shown to be inadequate—perhaps we will be forced to admit that evil cannot be explained by anything other than itself, and hence any reductionist account misleads.

We ask the voluntarist to explain human wrong-doing. How do we make sense of a criminal, for example, killing his victim to keep him from revealing an embarrassing secret? It is the killer's free will, they say; that explains it. This seems intuitively acceptable. We ask further: how do we make sense of human virtue? Explain, we ask, the loving saint's remarkable sacrifice in feeding the hungry and comforting the afflicted. Again, it is the saint's free will that explains it. This too, seems intuitively sound. But we reflect on these answers. The free will explains both good and evil; it explains both kindness and cruelty, promise-breaking and promise-keeping. There is a vague disquiet. What does it mean to explain? Do we explain the rock going up in the air the same way we explain the rock going down? If the latter is explained by gravity, do we say gravity also explains the former? We seem to be cheated of our expectations. Presumably explanations should somehow account for the differences between opposites. Else why explain at all?

Suppose the child asks us to explain the rain, and we respond with the words: the weather. When asked to explain the sunny day, we respond with the same words: the weather. In some sense, of course, both sunny days and rainy days are part of the broader phenomenon, weather. But weather is explained by rain and sun, not the other way around. We make this point to the voluntarist, who responds: in the case of immorality the free will submits to the lure of base instincts; in the case of morality the will responds to the noble instincts. This suggests, however, that the difference between the moral and the immoral rests on the more fundamental difference between good instincts and bad instincts. Why even bring in the will? It is not the good or bad instincts that matter, responds the voluntarist, but our *choice* of them. We nod, perhaps; relieved.

But in both cases we choose. So it cannot be the choice that makes them good or bad, unless there is bad choosing not dependent on bad choices and good choosing not dependent on good choices. Perhaps there are two free wills, the good will choosing good and the bad will choosing bad. The voluntarist is appalled: there is but one will, capable of choosing good or bad. Perhaps so, but we are asking what accounts for the difference, and the voluntarist insists that the difference *is* accounted for by the single will. This is akin to the broad abstraction "weather" accounting for rainy and sunny days. It does not satisfy.

Are these convolutions reason enough to abandon the voluntarist altogether and accede to the determinists? They tell us the liar was determined to lie and the truth-teller was determined to tell the truth. What good is that? Determinism is no better than voluntarism in explaining what we want to know, but it is much worse than voluntarism in that it renders morality a sub-species of mechanism and hence all vivid sense of the "ought" is lost, in spite of the compatabilist's attempts to paper over the cracks. Furthermore, the determinist employs the metaphysical presupposition of inevitability, which itself is counter to the possibility of being a person, and hence, when applied to persons, is the logic of evil. Both voluntaristic and deterministic metaphysics fail us; for they both insist on deriving evil, goodness, and badness from something else: either a machine-like world grinding out little entities akin to a mill-stone crushing grains to powder, or entities like wills that vanish into mysteries when put to actual, explanative use. They both assume that an ontology of entities must somehow be presupposed; but such an assumption always and ever overlooks the assumer. They thus both assume a non-personal world into which persons later are somehow added, trying to explain the latter by reference to the former, a task doomed to failure. The mechanist's belief that "complexity" somehow covers the gap between organisms and moral agency is just as much a superstition as the belief that imps like Robin Goodfellow knock over the milk. It is not that there is no evidence lurking in the mangle of complexity; it is rather there can be no evidence. Yet the reality of evil persists. Both deterministic "complexities" and voluntaristic "wills" are like astronomical black holes: they absorb everything into themselves, and produce no light at all.

We must begin where we are. We cannot begin by some retrograde projection of a world lacking persons that "somehow" explains persons, since "explaining" itself is entirely dependent on the reality of persons. Even evolution, which may well be the greatest scientific theory ever, cannot explain, through its chief principle of adaptability by mutations, the capacity to make moral judgments. We are, indeed, not asking the questions of our origins as a species, but simply what it means to be moral and what it means to be agents or victims of evil; and what, if anything, distinguishes the two. In these questions we transcend our species. I am not reducible to my species. If, however, the question is not about our mechanistic or evolutionary origins, nor even the metaphysical status of our free will, and if we "must begin where we are"—that is: this side of evil—how can we interrogate ourselves? The formal principle that must be exposed as false is that one must judge "systems" or even actual people concerning bad and evil, only from *outside* the system or the act of judging. This dubious principle is originally maintained as a proviso against bigotry: the fox should not guard the chickens. Mafia criminals should not be on the juries considering Mafia criminals. Practical wisdom does indeed dictate a need for non-biased judgment, often disastrously called "objectivity," but to press this beyond the concerns about bias is itself a bias. There are as many counter-intuitions suggesting that only the familiar should judge their own kind as there are intuitions that only outsiders can judge them. Former drug-abusers may be the best teachers against abuse, parents struggling with adolescents may be the best judges of the anguish inherent in this strain on families. Surely we do not claim only non-swimmers can teach us to swim. Indeed the whole point behind the near-sacred phase of common-law countries, "a jury of your peers" means exactly that only those who are within a culture can judge those who abuse its laws. We thus find ourselves already in the world, beleaguered by fate, evil, guilt, and our own responsibility. Since questions that focus on entities cannot help, nor questions of origins, nor questions of extra-cultural tribunals trying to judge cultures, we must ask, as we have been doing, what it means for evil to be real; and what it means for evil to be distinguished from bad.

Two distinct questions seem to merge, yet clash. On the one hand our extensive inquiries suggest that evil is that prior reality that ultimately grounds all moral and ethical judgments. Evil is not based on the reality of the soul or the will or God or the body or any other entity; evil itself is real, and is not derived from anything else. On the other hand, these same inquiries have supported a clear demarcation between evil and the other censures of worth and value, such as wickedness, immorality, misfortune and injustice. This presents a problem. If evil is the reality that grounds all judgments of worth, how can we understand evil as radically distinct from immorality? Are not the two discoveries—first, that evil alone among what is censured is real, and as such grounds all other censure; and second, that evil is entirely distinct from other censures—are they not inconsistent? If they are not inconsistent—and they are not—how do we nevertheless think them together?

It is indeed because evil alone among the censures is real that it must be distinct from them. Throughout this adventure many descriptions of evil have emerged from the analyses of our own existential phenomena. We have noted, for example, that evil seems non-purposive, that it seem coldly dispassionate, that it threatens from without, that it seems impersonal in the sense of anti-human, that it is greater than undeserved suffering. In the analysis of the unholy it was revealed that evil has the quality—perhaps even the essential quality—of inevitability, contrasting with the non-inevitability of persons. In all of these discoveries evil is contrasted with what makes us persons—even those faults and errors that make us persons. Human weakness, and the dreadful consequences of unchecked desires, though thoroughly reprehensible, nevertheless belong to us as persons; whereas evil threatens the very possibility of being persons. So how can the latter be the metaphysical basis of the former, and still be distinct?

It is possible for a person to be immoral without being an agent of evil, just as one can break the laws of one's country without being a traitor. But every breakage nevertheless undermines the respect for law, which in turn offends the reality of the nation that binds us together as a people, without which being a person would not be possible. So just as treason is on one level a mere crime among other crimes, it also attacks the very reality that makes crime possible at all. Yet, any and every non-treasonous crime is somehow grounded in what treason *means*: the attack against the institution that makes crimes and punitive justice possible. Ordinary moral violations are not evil; they are grounded in the reality of persons, who in turn *are* persons because of the struggle with good and evil. It is dangerous to depict evil as so rare and spectacular that it is seen as alien to our reality. Evil, as the metaphysical ground of all censure is ubiquitous; to confront it is what it means to be good.

What we call evil in the spectacular sense, however, is the external manifestation of the true target of its venom: the ability to be a person; and as such, must be seen as the outstanding, at times perhaps latent, threat that looms as a forfeit of our possibility. In this precise sense, evil is confronted as a non-reducible reality that nevertheless seeks to disguise itself.

We are responsible for what we do. Metaphysical accounts of this, such as the claim we "have" a free will, are meant to explain this responsibility by appeals to a deeper or more fundamental reality. Whether such metaphysical attempts succeed or fail is perhaps moot, but in any event cannot be seen as a source of dubiety about our being responsible. Aristotle's account of gravity may have been proven false, but we do not thereby deny that things fall. The phrase 'free will' may be a mere semantic locus for spotting the proper language to deal with the truth of our moral reality. That we ought not abuse children, however, does not hinge upon the success of the metaphysical effort, noble though it be. Similarly, there are indeed barbarians at the gate, cruelties beyond measure, genuine assaults against our being able to be persons, and ills of such monument and moment that only magnificence can thwart. These are evil. It is because truth matters in order to be a person that we not only must war against specific enemies, but also wage against our own ignorance of the enemy's reality, and indeed our own reality. Philosophical learning is thus a part of our life-sustaining struggle.

We are not only a witness to the unspeakable, we are also a part of it. The redemption lies in letting the unspeakable speak.

Epilogue

"... God so commanded, and left that command
Sole daughter of his voice; the rest, we live
Law to ourselves; our reason is our law."
(Milton, *Paradise Lost*, IX, 652-4)

Will we ever truly understand this? The last five words contrast so vividly with the first three it seems they can never be reconciled. If our morality is based upon our reason, then why should we ever obey anything that is a mere command, even from God, if it is unsupported by thought or analysis? For the moral rationalist, obedience based solely on external authority has no legitimate claim upon us. Indeed, what is often called "blind obedience" is seen as the canker that destroys the rose; it explains the Nazis, the Communists and the burners of heretics; it also explains the dreary mindlessness of human drones who, slave-like, follow the precepts of their culture solely out of fearful obedience, an image that depresses even were all the precepts morally sound.

In this passage, Eve speaks to Satan explaining why she should not eat of the forbidden tree. The nutrition gained from eating of its fruit is the knowledge of good and evil. The paradoxes inherent in this are reeling. Is the violation of a sacred command, unreachable by mere moral reasoning, the true, perhaps only, *evil*? Is it evil only because it violates divine command, and not at all the moral law available by human thought? If so, is it not irrational to obey? These reflections suggest that perhaps pure, unquestioned obedience is a species of slave morality. But is it always? Were the ill-fed Eve to look back after her fall, might she not say: I should have obeyed the unreasoned command of God simply because I loved him, not because it was required? This appeal to obedience based on love rather than duty changes everything. Perhaps, however, this kind of loving is simply not possible for the innocent. Milton's God, too, may have looked back with relief and pride in his daughter, Eve, for completing the act of her creation by becoming free, and hence non-innocent.

We are the new, though unsavory, innocents, as eunuchs must be innocent of rape or slaves must be innocent by the sheer debasement of being a slave. In this new and ugly innocence we are cheated of the language that redeems; we can sin no more since 'sin' is excised from our language and evil is demoted as superstition. We have returned to a polluted Eden, bereft even of a serpent to tempt us. We have vomited out the poison of the forbidden fruit, fouling the ground; but these abdominal wretchings have left us wretches. The irony of our fate may well be that, for all our sophistication, we have forgotten what Eve paid so dearly for us to have: the knowledge of good and evil.

Marquette Studies in Philosophy
Andrew Tallon, Editor
Standing orders accepted
* denotes available as e-book

1.* Harry Klocker, S.J. *William of Ockham and the Divine Freedom*
ISBN 0-87462-001-5. 141 pages, pp., index. $15. Second edition, reviewed, corrected and with a new Introduction.
2.* Margaret Monahan Hogan. *Finality and Marriage*
ISBN 0-87462-600-5. 122 pp. Paper. $15.
3.* Gerald A. McCool, S.J. *The Neo-Thomists*
ISBN 0-87462-601-1. 175 pp. Paper. $20.
4.* Max Scheler. *Ressentiment*
ISBN 0-87462-602-1. 172 pp. Paper. $20. New Introduction by Manfred S. Frings.
5.* Knud Løgstrup. *Metaphysics.* Translated by Dr. Russell Dees
ISBN 0-87462-603-X. Volume I, 342 pp. Paper. $35.
ISBN 0-67462-607-2. Volume II, 402 pp. Paper. $40. Two volume set priced at $70.
6. Howard P. Kainz. *Democracy and the "Kingdom of God"*
ISBN 0-87462-610-2. 250 pp. Paper. $25.
7.* Manfred Frings. *Max Scheler. A Concise Introduction into the World of a Great Thinker*
ISBN 0-87462-605-6. 200 pp. Paper. $20. Second ed., rev. New Foreword by the author.
8.* G. Heath King. *Existence Thought Style: Perspectives of a Primary Relation, portrayed through the work of Søren Kierkegaard.* English edition by Timothy Kircher.
ISBN 0-87462-606-4. 187 pp., index. Paper. $20.
9. Augustine Shutte. *Philosophy for Africa*
ISBN 0-87462-608-0. 184 pp. Paper. $20.
10.* Paul Ricoeur. *Key to Husserl's Ideas I.* Translated by Bond Harris and Jacqueline Bouchard Spurlock.With a Foreword by Pol Vandevelde.
ISBN 0-87462-609-9. 176 pp., index. Paper. $20.
11. Karl Jaspers. *Reason and Existenz.* With an Afterword by Pol Vandevelde.
ISBN 0-87462-611-0. 180 pp. Paper. $20.
12. *Gregory R. Beabout. *Freedom and Its Misuses: Kierkegaard on Anxiety and Despair*
ISBN 0-87462-612-9. 192 pp., index. Paper. $20.

14.* Manfred S. Frings. *The Mind of Max Scheler. The First Comprehensive Guide Based on the Complete Works*
   ISBN 0-87462-613-7. 328 pp. Paper. $35.
15.* Claude Pavur. *Nietzsche Humanist*
   ISBN 0-87462-614-5. 214 pp., index. Paper. $25.
16.* Pierre Rousselot. *Intelligence: Sense of Being, Faculty of God.* Translation if *L'Intellectualismse de saint Thomas* with a Foreword and Notes by Andrew Tallon.
   ISBN 0-87462-615-3. xxxvi + 240 pp., index. Paper. $30.
17.* Immanuel Kant. *Critique of Practical Reason.* Translation by H.W. Cassirer. Edited by G. Heath King and Ronald Weitzman and with an Introduction by D.M. MacKinnon.
   ISBN 0-87462-616-1. Paper. 218 pp. $20.
18.* *Gabriel Marcel's Perspectives on The Broken World.* Translated by Katharine Rose Hanley. *The Broken World,* A Four-Act Play followed by "Concrete Approaches to Investigating the Ontological Mystery." Six orignal illustrations by Stephen Healy. Commentaries by Henri Gouhier and Marcel Belay. Eight Appendices. Introduction by Ralph McInerny. Bibliographies. Indexes.
   ISBN 0-87462-617-X. paperbound. 242 pp. $25.
20. Karl-Otto Apel. *Towards a Transformation of Philosophy.* With a new Foreword by Pol Vandevelde.
   ISBN 0-87462-619-6. Paper. 308 pp. $35.
22.* Michael Gelven. *This Side of Evil.*
   ISBN 0-87462-621-8. Paper. 162 pp. $20.

Marquette Studies in Theology
Andrew Tallon, Editor
Standing orders accepted
* denotes available as e-book

1.* Frederick M. Bliss. *Understanding Reception*
   ISBN 0-87462-625-0. 180 pp., index, bibliography. Paper. $20.
2.* Martin Albl, Paul Eddy, Renée Mirkes, OSF, Editors. *Directions in New Testament Methods*
   ISBN 0-87462-626-9. 129 pp. Annotated bibliography. Paper. $15. Foreword by William S. Kurz.
3.* Robert M. Doran. *Subject and Psyche*
   ISBN 0-87462-627-7. 285 pp. Paper. $25. Second ed., rev. With a new Foreword by the author.

4.* Kenneth Hagen, editor. *The Bible in the Churches. How Various Christians Interpret the Scriptures*
ISBN 0-87462-628-5. 218 pp. Paper. $25. Third, revised editon. New chapter on Reformed tradition. Index.

5.* Jamie T. Phelps, O.P., Editor. *Black and Catholic: The Challenge and Gift of Black Folk. Contributions of..... African American Experience and Thought to Catholic Theology*
ISBN 0-87462-629-3. 182 pp. Index. Paper. $20. Foreword by Patrick Carey.

6. *Karl Rahner. *Spirit in the World.* New, Corrected Translation by William Dych. Foreword by Francis Fiorenza.
ISBN 0-87462-630-7. COMPUTER DISK VERSION. $10. Available on 3.5 inch disk; specify Macintosh or Windows. By a special arrangement with Continuum Publishing Co.

7.* Karl Rahner. *Hearer of the Word.* New Translation of the First Edition by Joseph Donceel. Edited and with anIntroduction by Andrew Tallon. By a special arrangement with Continuum Publishing Co.
ISBN 0-87462-631-5. COMPUTER DISK VERSION. Autumn, 1994. $10. Available on 3.5 inch disk; specify Macintosh orWindows.

8.* Robert M. Doran. *Theological Foundations. Vol. 1 Intentionality and Psyche*
ISBN 0-87462-632-3. 484 pp. Paper. $50.

9.* Robert M. Doran. *Theological Foundations. Vol. 2 Theology and Culture*
ISBN 0-87462-633-1. 533 pp. Paper. $55.

10.* Patrick W. Carey. *Orestes A. Brownson: A Bibliography, 1826-1876*
ISBN 0-87462-634-X. 212 pp. Index. Paper. $25.

11.* John Martinetti, S.J. *Reason to Believe Today*
ISBN 0-87462-635-8. 216 pp. Paper. $25.

12.* George H. Tavard. *Trina Deitas: The Controversy between Hincmar and Gottschalk*
ISBN 0-87462-636-6. 160 pp. Paper. $20.

13.* Jeanne Cover, IBVM. *Love–The Driving Force. Mary Ward's Spirituality. Its Significance for Moral Theology*
ISBN 0-87462-637-4. 217 pp. Paper. $25.

14.* David A. Boileau, Editor. *Principles of Catholic Social Teaching*
ISBN 0-87462-638-2. 204 pp. Paper. $25.

15.* Michael Purcell. *Mystery and Method: The Other in Rahner and Levinas.* With a Foreword by Andrew Tallon.
ISBN 0-87462-639-0. Paper. 394 pp. $45.

17.* *Catholic Theology in the University: Source of Wholeness.* Virginis M. Shaddy, editor.
ISBN 0-87462-641-2. Paper. 120 pp. $15.